From Standards to Success

A Guide for School Leaders

Mark R. O'Shea

Association for Supervision and Curriculum Development
Alexandria, Virginia USA

Association for Supervision and Curriculum Development
1703 N. Beauregard St. • Alexandria, VA 22311-1714 USA
Phone: 800-933-2723 or 703-578-9600 • Fax: 703-575-5400
Web site: www.ascd.org • E-mail: member@ascd.org
Author guidelines: www.ascd.org/write

Gene R. Carter, *Executive Director;* Nancy Modrak, *Director of Publishing;* Julie Houtz, *Director of Book Editing & Production;* Genny Ostertag, *Project Manager;* Shelley Kirby, *Graphic Designer;* Circle Graphics, *Typesetter;* Tracey A. Franklin, *Production Manager*

All Web links in this book are correct as of the publication date below but may have become inactive or otherwise modified since that time. If you notice a deactivated or changed link, please e-mail books@ascd.org with the words "Link Update" in the subject line. In your message, please specify the Web link, the book title, and the page number on which the link appears.

ASCD Member Book, No. FY05-08 (July 2005, PC). ASCD Member Books mail to Premium (P), Comprehensive (C), and Regular (R) members on this schedule: Jan., PC; Feb., P; Apr., PCR; May, P; July, PC; Aug., P; Sept., PCR; Nov., PC; Dec., P.

Paperback ISBN: 1-4166-0207-0 • ASCD product #105017

e-books: retail PDF ISBN 1-4166-0291-7 • netLibrary ISBN 1-4166-0289-5 • ebrary ISBN 1-4166-0290-9

Quantity discounts for this book: 10–49 copies, 10%; 50+ copies, 15%; for 500 or more copies, call 800-933-2723, ext. 5634, or 703-575-5634.

Library of Congress Cataloging-in-Publication Data

O'Shea, Mark R., 1946-
    From standards to success : a guide for school leaders / Mark R. O'Shea.
        p. cm.
    Includes bibliographical references and index.
    ISBN 1-4166-0207-0 (alk. paper)
    1. Education—Standards—United States—Handbooks, manuals, etc. 2. Curriculum planning—United States—Standards—Handbooks, manuals, etc. 3. Educational leadership—United States. I. Title.

    LB3060.83.O84 2005
    379.1'58—dc22

                                                                    2005009481

12 11 10 09 08 07 06 05   12 11 10 9 8 7 6 5 4 3 2 1

To my wife, Lorraine, a great teacher,
to my daughters, Kelly and Lindsey,
and to Howard Kimmel, for the many years of partnership
for the improvement of teaching and learning.

From
Standards
to Success

A Guide for School Leaders

Figure List vi

Preface ix

Acknowledgments xiii

Chapter 1: A Visit to a Standards-Based School 1

Chapter 2: An Overview of Curriculum Management for
Standards Achievement 15

Chapter 3: The Standards Achievement Planning Cycle 45

Chapter 4: The District's Plans for Standards Implementation 62

Chapter 5: The Principal's Role in a Standards-Based School 89

Chapter 6: Evaluation of Standards Achievement 106

Chapter 7: Professional Development for Standards
Achievement 130

Afterword 150

Notes 153

Bibliography 156

Index 159

About the Author 162

Figure List

1.1 Standards-Based Lesson Plan for 2nd Grade Science............. 3

1.2 Checklist of Practices in a Standards-Based School 13

2.1 Common Strategies for Implementing Standards.................... 20

2.2 Standards-Based Teaching as a "Black Box" Problem 21

2.3 Typical Lesson Plan for 3rd Grade Social Studies................... 27

2.4 Lesson Plan for 3rd Grade Social Studies with
     Standards Statement 29

2.5 Standards-Based Lesson Plan for 3rd Grade
     Social Studies... 30

2.6 Enabling Conditions for Meeting the Standards...................... 36

2.7 Checklist of Local Standards Implementation Efforts 43

3.1 Bloom's Taxonomy of Educational Objectives with
     Behavioral Verbs 53

3.2 Objectives and Activities of the Lesson Plan for
     2nd Grade Science 57

3.3 Checklist for Adopting the Planning Cycle............................... 60

4.1 Model Agenda for Standards-Based Reform 68

4.2 Nominal Alignment in a Curriculum Guide 78

4.3 Curriculum Guide Focused on Standards Achievement.......... 79

4.4   Curriculum Guide with Standards Achievement Dates 80

4.5   Components of Effective Curriculum Guides and
       Planning Resources 83

4.6   Checklist for Standards Implementation at the
       District Level 87

5.1   Expectations for Standards-Based Lesson Plans...................... 98

5.2   Criteria for Evaluating a Standards-Based Lesson 100

5.3   Checklist for Leading a Standards-Based School 104

6.1   Checklist for a History of Science Lesson 114

6.2   Student Benchmark Test Report.. 118

6.3   Classroom Benchmark Test Report.. 120

6.4   Checklist for a District Standards Assessment System 128

7.1   Agenda for Principal and Lead Teacher Training..................... 140

7.2   Agenda for Teacher Training... 142

7.3   Checklist for Professional Development Programs.................. 148

Preface

As we enter the second administration of President George W. Bush, the regulations of No Child Left Behind are affecting school districts all across the United States. States with large numbers of rural and language minority schools are in desperate need of highly qualified teachers. But the difficulty of finding such teachers for underperforming schools has always been with us. The new challenge is making adequate yearly progress in multiple measures of student achievement, but most notably in the achievement of state content standards.

Despite the urgency, school leaders and public policy experts continue to focus on national school reform movements that deal only tangentially with standards achievement. Of even greater concern is the lack of a prescription, or clear technology, for achieving the standards. Enabling conditions, resources, assessments, and all sorts of policies have been proposed related to standards implementation. The only missing element is explicit directions to teachers and administrators that, if followed, will lead to standards achievement. *From Standards to Success* provides the prescription.

Although other novel elements are included in this book, its central feature is the Standards Achievement Planning Cycle (SAPC). I propose this construct to all school leaders and teachers not as the final answer, but as the first proposal in a hoped-for sequence of increasingly effective mechanisms, or strategies, for achieving standards. I boldly contend that the SAPC is the first true theory of action for state standards implementation. It contains all the necessary elements of such a theory. It starts with the inputs to the system and specifically describes a process that engages the existing resources found, in some form, in almost every state: standards, frameworks, test blueprints, and other state standards documents. The SAPC, through a series of explicit actions, transforms the input resources into intermediate products that lead, one after the other, to standards achievement as the goal of daily instruction.

The SAPC has been tested by preservice teachers at California State University–Monterey Bay and by experienced teachers from California to New Jersey. It works because it brings together reform initiatives that have demonstrated improved teaching and learning in their own right. These include Japanese Lesson Study, early revelations of the New Standards Project, Looking at Student Work, and outcomes-based teaching.

So how can we not feel hopeful? A mechanism for meeting the standards is finally available. The real problem, alas, is in sustaining its use. Collaborative lesson planning and student work evaluation need continuous encouragement and cultivation until they become habits of mind. Therefore, this book allocates relatively few pages to describing the elements of the SAPC and quite a few pages to discussing the enabling and sustaining conditions that will keep the SAPC unfolding in schools.

Perhaps the reader is in a position of influence over state policy involving academic content standards. If so, I hope that the SAPC recommendations will help lead to state policy reform. In too many settings, the policy environment is inconsistent and incoherent. In some states, including California, policy seems to invite failure rather than success. The insistence on achievement of an excessive number of standards and the refusal to rank standards by significance is not helpful. In California, standardized tests are still used to rate or compare districts. There is no need for any state or district to administer a standardized test as long as the National Assessment of Educational Progress can serve its role of comparing the academic rigor of state standards.

The reliance of state policymakers on curriculum alignment and text adoption only demonstrates that policymakers do not understand how a teacher should function differently in a standards-based classroom. Moreover, it is unfair to expect results from teachers without defining a process that they can use to achieve the desired results. *From Standards to Success* focuses on the processes that can be used to achieve the standards.

Acknowledgments

This book began with the recognition that teachers need help achieving standards. Standards, frameworks, and curriculum resources, although necessary, are not sufficient to help teachers meet the expectations of the standards.

I want to thank Howard Kimmel and the staff of the Center for Pre-college Programs at the New Jersey Institute of Technology for offering their support, for involving me in their mission, and for giving me the opportunity to work with many dedicated, inspiring teachers in New Jersey's urban centers.

Thanks to the many preservice and inservice teachers in New Jersey and California who have helped me refine the Standards Achievement Planning Cycle (SAPC), including my colleagues at Watsonville High School and Alisal High School, especially Pat and Bakari. And thanks to all the teachers in the various summer institutes, from the central ward of Newark to Beverly Hills. I would also like to thank the many school leaders who have invited me into their districts to work and converse with their teachers, who ultimately taught me more than I taught them. Thanks to Rex Comer, Mike Melton, Candy McCarthy, Joe Jaconette, Bob Martinez, and everyone in Union City, Newark, and Harrison.

As a professor with varied responsibilities and obligations, I have been able to persist in preparing this book because of the assistance I have received from colleagues and staff who have helped me with so many other tasks. Thank you, Catherine, Sophia, Delberta, and

Christina. And thank you, Michele, for your help with the final preparation and submission of the manuscript.

Thanks also to my wife, Lorraine, who inspired me to bring together so many experiences to create the story of the La Senda School District. This fictional entity is an amalgam of promising developments arising all over the United States. Thanks to my daughter Lindsey who helped me edit the early drafts of this work, and to my daughter Kelly for her encouragement.

Finally, I would like to acknowledge the support and assistance of the National Science Foundation and the U.S. Department of Education through their funding of projects in New Jersey and California where the SAPC evolved.

1

A Visit to a Standards-Based School

In the fall of 1989, President George H. W. Bush presided over a U.S. education summit for state governors in Charlottesville, Virginia. This historic meeting gave rise to state academic content standards that have displaced national curriculum standards in leading school reform in the United States. As a result of the meeting, power and influence over curriculum moved dramatically away from the local school districts and into state executive offices, state legislatures, and state departments of education. This sudden transfer of power from local school districts to state authorities was surprisingly short-lived. Before states could even formulate policies and procedures to use the power of their standards, their influence over curriculum was trumped by the federal government through the reauthorization of the Elementary and Secondary Education Act, now known as No Child Left Behind.

This new law requires states to use academic content standards to benchmark federally mandated "adequate yearly progress" toward ambitious school improvement goals. Despite continuing controversy, state content standards have emerged as the most powerful manifestation of the school reform that began with *A Nation at Risk* more than 20 years ago. Regardless of our views about the future of the standards, one essential fact remains steadfastly in place: Schools and districts that fail to demonstrate growth in standards achievement face sanctions. And they are likely to face them into the foreseeable future.

This book describes a comprehensive approach to implementing standards. The central strategy in this new approach includes elements of whole-school reform that are organized into a recursive cycle of instructional planning, teaching, and evaluation of students' work— all focused on raising learning expectations for standards achievement. The approach does not rely on widely used but ineffectual strategies, including curriculum alignment and text adoption procedures. These popular methods only ensure that topics in the standards are "covered." They do not raise expectations, as only teachers can do.

To illustrate this alternative approach, let us imagine that we are visiting a fictional elementary school near Los Angeles, California, where teachers use the recursive cycle of standards-based planning to raise expectations for standards achievement. We will see the classroom of a teacher who plans standards-based lessons with her grade-level team. Then we will explore strategies used by the principal and other school leaders to support teachers as they plan and teach lessons to meet the standards.

Looking into a Standards-Based Classroom

Following a brief welcome to Mariposa Elementary School by the principal, Mrs. Lewis, we are escorted to the classroom of Mrs. Hernandez, a 2nd grade teacher. Mrs. Hernandez works closely with other teachers at her grade level to plan standards-based lessons. She invites us to examine her lesson plan as we enter the classroom.

Mrs. Hernandez's lesson plan is provided in Figure 1.1, along with callouts identifying the elements of the plan that make it standards-based. The lesson objectives are particularly important. They are written as outcomes to be demonstrated by the students. Furthermore, the outcomes are written from 2nd grade science and language arts standards that the teacher is addressing in her lesson.

Using Standards to Focus Teaching

We finish our review of the lesson plan just as Mrs. Hernandez invites the children to a corner of the classroom to look at picture

FIGURE 1.1

Standards-Based Lesson Plan for 2nd Grade Science

Topic: Life cycles of organisms

Rationale: Plants and animals have life cycles that are characteristic of their species. Some animal groups have distinctive life cycle stages.

Content Standards:

Life Sciences
2. Plants and animals have predictable life cycles.
   b. *Students know* the sequential stages of life cycles are different for different animals, such as butterflies, frogs, and mice.[1]

Investigation and Experimentation
4. Scientific progress is made by asking meaningful questions and conducting careful investigations.
   d. Students will write or draw descriptions of a sequence of steps, events, and observations.[2]

Writing
2.1 Students write brief narratives based on their experiences:
   a. Move through a logical sequence of events.
   b. Describe the setting, characters, objects, and events in detail.[3]

Standards focus the lesson on specific learning to be accomplished.

Objectives: In this lesson we examine the life cycles of frogs and butterflies. The life cycles of other animals, including mice, will be addressed at another time. For today:
• Given pictures of the life cycle stages of frogs and butterflies, students *will place* them in proper order for each animal.
• Students *will list* the life cycle stages of frogs and butterflies in proper order.
• In a brief skit about the life of a frog or a butterfly, students *will describe* the features of the life cycle stage they are portraying.
• Following a reading of *The Very Hungry Caterpillar*, students *will write* a description of themselves growing up as a frog or a butterfly. They *will use* proper stage names and the academic language of the standards in their description.

The teacher describes what students will do to meet the selected standards for this lesson. Verbs are italicized, emphasizing the observable nature of expected student outcomes.

(continued)

FIGURE 1.1   (continued)

Materials:

- Activity cards showing the life cycle stages of frogs and butterflies on one side and information about each stage on the other side
- Video of the growth and development of the frog and the butterfly from egg to adult
- A copy of the children's book *The Very Hungry Caterpillar*

Activities:

1. Show frog and butterfly activity cards; ask students to identify the animals; see whether students know any life cycle stages and their names.
2. Using the activity cards, reveal all stages of both animals in proper order; elicit student choral recitations of each stage name as it appears.
3. Show a video of the growth and development of the frog and the butterfly.
4. Have pairs of students sort shuffled activity cards into proper order for each animal.
5. Have pairs of students write a list of the life cycle stages in proper order for each animal, working from sorted picture cards.
6. Have several students line up in sequential order of the life cycle stages for each animal and ask them to describe the particular stage they are portraying. They will say what the animal eats and where it lives.

These activities should lead students to demonstrate the outcomes stated in the objectives.

Assessment:

Read *The Very Hungry Caterpillar* to all students in reading circle. Following the reading of the story, students *will write* their own story about growing up as a frog or a butterfly, using the words *stage* and *sequence* and naming each life cycle stage in proper order in their story.

The teacher will collect the students' work and examine each story to see that stage names appear in proper order.

cards of an adult frog and an adult butterfly. Several children raise their hands as they recognize these animals. Next, Mrs. Hernandez shows pictures of a cocoon and a tadpole. Only one or two children seem to recognize these life cycle stages. A discussion of each of the life cycle stages follows, with children providing choral responses to the teacher's questions. Mrs. Hernandez calls on several children to check their understanding:

Mrs. Hernandez:	Can anyone recall this early stage in the life of the butterfly?
Angelica:	That's the caterpillar.
Mrs. Hernandez:	Good, Angelica. And who can tell me what the tadpole will change into?

The conversation in the classroom includes the academic vocabulary of the standard selected for the lesson plan. Students use the words *stage, life cycle,* and *sequence.* The teacher knows that these terms and concepts are important components of the standard. Students will need to recognize and use them properly to demonstrate achievement of the standard, both in class and during state standards tests when they encounter questions about life cycles.

Mrs. Hernandez proceeds from the picture card activity to video episodes that show a frog and a butterfly growing from egg to adult. At the end of the video, she asks students questions to see whether they can move beyond mere recognition of stage names to an understanding of the concept of a life cycle.

Mrs. Hernandez:	Do people grow up in the same way as butterflies, Billy?
Billy:	I don't think we grow in different stages.
Mrs. Hernandez:	Billy says that people do not grow in stages like butterflies. What does the word *stage* mean to you, Latisha?
Latisha:	A stage is what you look like before you change.
Mrs. Hernandez:	How many life cycle stages does a frog have, Monica?
Monica:	Three or four, I think. Let me see . . . egg, tadpole, froglet, and adult.

As a result of the teacher's thoughtful questioning, students generate original language that includes the vocabulary of the selected standard. They say the words *sequence* and *stage* and explain their meanings. They identify stages by name, and the teacher writes each stage name on the board.

It is evident that children are engaged in meaningful academic work. They do not conduct word searches, fill out sentence completion worksheets, or work on tasks unrelated to the learning objectives of the lesson. Classroom activities are clearly aimed toward the achievement of planned outcomes that appear in the objectives.

Building Standards Assessment into the Classroom Routine

Mrs. Hernandez organizes and facilitates student-centered learning activities for individuals, pairs, or small groups. Following the video, children work in pairs to sort picture cards into the proper order for a frog's life cycle and a butterfly's life cycle. This activity is intended to achieve the following lesson plan objective: "Given pictures of the life cycle stages of frogs and butterflies, students *will place* them in proper order for each animal." The children identify stage names correctly as the teacher moves among the pairs, listening to their responses. Clearly, students are achieving this objective of the lesson plan.

While students are busy with the picture card activity, Mrs. Hernandez checks individuals' understanding. She is listening for proper use of the academic vocabulary and language of the standard. She is also looking for the card placement skills described in the lesson's objectives. The card placement skills anticipate the next objective to be demonstrated: "Students *will list* the life cycle stages of frogs and butterflies in proper order."

As Mrs. Hernandez moves from one pair of students to another, she seeks accurate lists, proper positioning of cards, and rearrangement of the cards into proper sequence. She is looking for students to place the cards in a cycle, not in a straight line. Mrs. Hernandez checks students' understanding of facts and concepts by asking questions, seeking clarification of responses, and requesting an alternative explanation or point of view. She is continually thinking about what students are saying, writing, or doing in relation to the specific behaviors described in the objectives of the lesson plan.

Following the sorting activity, Mrs. Hernandez asks one group of students to form a line in the front of the classroom with each child holding a picture card of a stage in a frog's life cycle. She asks the children to line up in the order of the frog's growth and to describe the particular stage they are portraying, including what their animal eats and where it lives. Following this brief skit, another group of students forms a properly sequenced line with butterfly picture cards. Students in this group take turns describing the life cycle stage of their pictured animal.

Measuring Achievement of Lesson Objectives

Soon Mrs. Hernandez gathers the children in a corner of the classroom to hear the story of *The Very Hungry Caterpillar* (Carle, 2001). Following the reading of the story, she asks students to write their own personal biographies as if they were butterflies or frogs growing up near the school. Their biographies must include the words *sequence* and *stage,* as well as the names of each of the life cycle stages of their selected animal in proper order.

Mrs. Hernandez intends to share the students' stories with her grade-level colleagues in their next planning meeting. During this meeting, the teachers will compare samples of their students' work with the standards-based objectives in the lesson plans. Mrs. Hernandez hopes that the story writing will lead students to demonstrate higher-level reasoning and thinking skills through the creative exercise of imagining themselves as butterflies or frogs. To close the lesson, Mrs. Hernandez reviews the activities of the day and asks the children to respond to her questions covering most of the lesson's objectives.

Reflecting on a Standards-Based Lesson

A teacher who has followed a standards-based lesson plan can reflect on her teaching in relation to the goals she sets for her students. Mrs. Hernandez can describe in detail the characteristics of the accurate, standards-meeting responses that students are expected to provide. She knows the distinctions between substandard and standards-meeting work because the objectives include descriptions of a proficient performance: "Given pictures of the life cycle stages of frogs and butterflies, students *will place* them in proper order for each animal."

Building Standards Assessment into Lesson Design

When teachers plan standards-based lessons by writing objectives in outcomes language, they learn to look beyond students' good behavior or enjoyment of the lesson for important indications of learning. Mrs. Hernandez has embedded several classroom assessments into her lesson to assure herself that students have achieved the important knowledge and skills specified in the standards. When the lesson is over, she examines students' work to see whether the objectives have been achieved. The lesson objectives are written directly from the state standards and frameworks. If students achieve the objectives of the lesson, they also achieve the selected standards.

Planning Work from Standards and Frameworks

Mrs. Hernandez's use of academic vocabulary reflects her deep understanding of the language and the content of the state frameworks and standards. During the lesson, she is careful to encourage students to use the important vocabulary of the standards. Her expectations come from reviewing the content of the standards and frameworks in regularly scheduled meetings with her colleagues. As a result of careful planning and collaboration with her grade-level team, Mrs. Hernandez can describe specific instances of achievement of critical components of California's science and language arts standards for 2nd grade students. She explains what happens in her classroom in relation to clear expectations for student learning described in the standards and frameworks.

Collaborating to Plan Lessons and Evaluate Students' Work

At Mariposa Elementary School, teachers plan their standards-based lessons in grade-level teams. They also use this time to compare students' work with the expectations of the standards.

Following the life cycles lesson, Mrs. Hernandez takes samples of her students' work to her grade-level team meeting, where the teachers review the objectives of the plan they designed together. Mrs. Hernandez discusses the events of the lesson, and she seeks her colleagues' opinions about the quality of the students' work in relation to the lesson's objectives and the standards. Examples of high-quality work that meet or exceed the standards will be retained for future teaching and used to set expectations for student learning from one year to the next. Ideally, expectations for achievement will rise over time as teachers review increasingly better examples of students' work before they teach the lessons in subsequent years. When teachers set their sights high by examining exemplary work samples, they establish a clearer learning target for all students.

Leading Standards Implementation for Teachers

Several changes in teacher roles and responsibilities must take place before teaching can improve in a standards-based school. Mrs. Hernandez and her colleagues did not always teach in a collaborative manner. Before they learned to plan together, they spent individual planning time looking at curriculum materials and producing activity sheets. For the most part, they developed lessons from published curriculum materials that they thought were aligned with the standards. After teaching, they checked response sheets for completion and accuracy. Lessons were deemed successful if students enjoyed them, were well behaved during instruction, and turned in completed exercises. The teachers did not have the resources or time to check students' work in relation to the standards.

The new planning and teaching behaviors at Mariposa Elementary School arose from a comprehensive school district reform process that included principals, curriculum coordinators, and central office administrators. Mrs. Lewis, the school principal, designed the staff development program in collaborative lesson planning with colleagues from the La Senda School District office. The program focused on instructional planning and the use of state standards, frameworks, and the district's updated curriculum guides. Teachers learned how to plan lessons that included explicit learning outcomes derived from standards documents. They learned how to select curriculum resources based on the usefulness of the resource for meeting instructional objectives. Finally, they learned to evaluate students' work by comparing it with the expectations of the standards, by embedding assessment in lesson activities, and by carefully evaluating work samples with colleagues.

After considerable practice with standards-based planning, teachers were required to submit their lesson plans for Mrs. Lewis's review. She checked the plans to see that the objectives included well-described student outcomes written from the standards and frameworks. Before long, lesson plans written from standards and frameworks became the primary tool for standards achievement, rather than textbooks and curriculum materials selected for topical alignment with the standards.

Making Adjustments to Support Standards Achievement

Adjustments had to be made to the daily and weekly schedule of school activities to accommodate collaborative lesson planning. Grade-level teams needed time to jointly plan standards-based lessons and analyze students' work. Mrs. Lewis introduced the additional planning time as the professional development workshops were taking place. After teachers became comfortable with the new planning procedures, the principal sat in on grade-level team meetings. She knew from her own training that the process of setting learning expectations for students calls for professional judgment, and she looked forward to these team meetings to contribute her own views as an educator.

The principal took additional actions to advocate for standards achievement. Essential language arts standards were posted in the school's main office and on bulletin boards in the hallway. Parents were informed about the essential standards at sessions during back-to-school night. Conversations with teachers and students included questions about their efforts to teach and understand important standards that were highlighted during the school year.

Emphasizing Standards During Classroom Observations

After teachers planned lessons together for more than a year, Mrs. Lewis began to use standards-based criteria to evaluate instruction during the supervision process. She asks teachers to submit their lesson plans to her before a scheduled observation. She expects the lessons to include objectives with outcome behaviors written from the standards. She also expects to see essential academic vocabulary from the frameworks and higher-level reasoning tasks in planned activities.

During her classroom visits, Mrs. Lewis looks for student learning behaviors and products described in the objectives of the lesson plan. Whereas many observers might focus on the actions of the teacher and the deportment of the students during the lesson, Mrs. Lewis also assesses whether students are able to produce standards-meeting work as described in the lesson plan.

After she completes lesson observations, Mrs. Lewis asks the teachers to evaluate their students' class work in relation to the lesson's objectives and to bring samples of evaluated work to their post-observation conferences.

Conducting Postobservation Conferences

During postobservation conferences, Mrs. Lewis and her teachers review the lesson and how it was designed to achieve specific content standards. The conference includes a discussion of the lesson's objectives and the student behaviors and products that were expected to result from instruction. Following the review of the plan, Mrs. Lewis examines samples of students' work. The teachers explain the extent to which the student performances described in the objectives are evident in the work samples. Mrs. Lewis asks questions about the work, the lesson's objectives, and how the objectives were written from the standards. Such conversations about standards-based lesson objectives and work samples help keep instruction focused on the standards and on student achievement.

Providing Management Support for School Districts

Mrs. Lewis does not rely solely on instructional supervision to assure herself that students are meeting the standards. She is confident that they are meeting the standards because teaching and learning in the La Senda School District are focused on standards achievement.

Evaluating the Curriculum

As the district trained principals in curriculum management for standards achievement, curriculum coordinators and lead teachers developed and installed curriculum pacing guides at the district level. Now teachers at each grade level know the critical standards they are expected to teach, the order in which they are to be achieved, and the approximate time to be spent in their achievement. They keep up with the pace of instruction described in the guide through grade-level collaborative planning.

The district also prepared for teacher success by installing a curriculum management plan. To achieve standards, schools must do more than merely select standards-aligned textbooks and align the curriculum with the subject matter of the standards. Many facets of instructional planning, teaching, and student learning must change. The principal and district administrators installed a management system that supports teachers as they follow a new protocol for team-based lesson planning and student work evaluation.

Developing Benchmark Testing

The district's benchmark-testing program measures student achievement of the standards at important intervals during the school year. Benchmark tests that emulate the format of state standards exams are administered in 40-minute sessions shortly after the deadline for the achievement of a specific set of standards. Teams of teachers developed the benchmark tests during summer curriculum planning time after lead teachers, working with district leaders, had selected and sequenced critical standards. Teachers wrote the benchmark test items from the critical standards found in the curriculum guide. They planned the distribution of items on the benchmark tests to match the distribution of items on state tests. A test-scoring system lets each teacher know the extent to which her students have mastered the learning expectations of the standards before state exams are administered in the spring.

Moreover, Mrs. Lewis and the other principals receive a report that profiles the performance of each classroom in their school within 48 hours of benchmark test administration. These reports indicate how each teacher is progressing with the standards. The benchmark testing complements the standards-based classroom observations in motivating teachers to sustain their collaborative activities. The teachers believe in the benchmark tests because teams of well-respected teachers wrote the test items from state standards, frameworks, and test blueprints.

Assessing Standards Implementation in Your School

The story of standards achievement at Mariposa Elementary School is intended to convey a vision of preferred practices within the current standards-based reform environment. This vision includes collaborative lesson planning and student work evaluation, along with the installation of a curriculum management system that supports teachers' efforts. The checklist presented in Figure 1.2 can be used to compare the planning, teaching, and administrative activities of any school with the practices described at the La Senda schools.

The checklist is not meant to include all promising reform activity in standards-based schools. Nor is it likely that any one school will exhibit all the listed activities. However, the checklist reflects practices that will help establish a curriculum management system to continuously measure and support achievement of state content standards at the classroom level. Similar checklists and curriculum auditing tools can be found at the end of each chapter.

FIGURE 1.2

Checklist of Practices in a Standards-Based School

Teachers

_____ have copies of standards and frameworks for each subject they teach.

_____ do not rely on unchallenging student desk work, including word searches, sentence completion exercises, puzzles, and other forms of response sheets not linked to standards.

_____ plan lessons from standards, frameworks, and related state documents.

(continued)

FIGURE 1.2   (continued)

Teachers (*continued*)

_____ plan standards-based lessons in regularly scheduled grade-level or subject-matter team meetings.

_____ submit standards-based lesson plans with objectives written from the standards to the principal for periodic review.

_____ examine student work samples in relation to the standards in regularly scheduled team meetings.

_____ retain copies of exemplary student work to use as benchmarks when teaching the lessons again.

Principals

_____ occasionally review samples of students' work to find evidence of state standards achievement.

_____ review standards-based lesson plans and resulting samples of students' work during instructional supervision.

_____ post critical standards in the teachers' lounge, the principal's office, and other school settings visited by parents and community members.

_____ have adjusted the school schedule of activities to accommodate grade-level team planning with the standards.

Districts

_____ have identified critical standards to be achieved in each subject for each grade level.

_____ have developed a curriculum pacing guide that informs teachers when their students should achieve critical standards throughout the school year.

_____ use benchmark tests to measure the achievement of important standards at quarterly intervals throughout the school year.

_____ use the benchmark assessment system to inform teachers of the progress that each of their students is making toward the achievement of critical standards likely to be assessed on annual standards-based tests.

2

An Overview of Curriculum Management for Standards Achievement

The teaching portrayed in Mrs. Hernandez's classroom in Chapter 1 does not arise from conventional responses to the standards mandate. This chapter will examine these conventional responses and their limitations and then introduce the protocol for planning lessons and evaluating students' work that helps Mrs. Hernandez and other teachers at Mariposa Elementary School achieve state standards in California. The protocol, called the Standards Achievement Planning Cycle (SAPC), links state standards to improved student achievement. The SAPC delineates the teacher's role in implementing the standards.

School districts need to install enabling conditions before teachers can succeed with the SAPC. In addition, a curriculum management system that supports teachers and helps them persist with the SAPC is an essential component of effective standards-based schools.

District Strategies for Meeting the Standards

Schools have progressed through a series of curriculum and teaching initiatives in their search for the right mix of strategies that will lead to student achievement of the standards. Although districts may select different approaches to the standards in any given year, a pattern of responses has emerged. The first response focused on alignment. School districts took action to ensure that teachers conveyed the skills and topics of the state standards. This first response involved one or more specific strategies, including alignment of the curriculum with the scope and sequence of the standards, adoption of standards-aligned curriculum materials, and development of teacher training programs in the content of the standards.

When this first step was completed, administrators expressed satisfaction that their districts were "standards-based" or "aligned with the standards." When No Child Left Behind became law, the increased accountability for standards achievement stimulated districts to formulate a second approach. These actions centered on the high-stakes tests rather than the content of the standards and frameworks. Administrators looked at the results of standards-based tests and focused teachers on test preparation.

In a few settings, there has been an additional response, which involves a more intensive focus on the alignment strategy. This recent approach attends to issues of curriculum pacing and progress assessment. In essence, it includes the application of tighter controls on what is taught in the classroom.

Aligning the Curriculum with the Standards

Perhaps the single most popular approach to the standards is curriculum alignment. Most school districts have worked hard to align the scope and sequence of the curriculum with the scope and sequence of topics in state standards.

Clearly, teachers need to cover the topics included in the standards, but this task alone is not enough. There is a distinct difference between alignment with the topics of the standards and achievement of the expectations included in the standards. Standards were written to raise expectations of students' intellectual engagement with the subject matter. These expectations include the acquisition of quantitative and qualitative reasoning skills and the understanding of complex concepts and principles. Mere topic coverage, or the alignment of topics described in two different documents, does not ensure achievement of the higher expectations described in state standards.

Adopting Standards-Aligned Curriculum Materials

Another popular approach to alignment is the textbook adoption process. District leaders justify this strategy through the use of a simple deduction: If adopted textbooks contain the knowledge and skills of the standards, then students will learn this information when teachers use these resources. District administrators can ask textbook adoption committees to use standards alignment as a criterion for selecting new texts. At least two problems result when districts rely on the adoption process, however: superficial coverage and inadequate pacing for standards achievement.

In California, elementary and middle school texts must be approved for local use through a state adoption process. The essential criterion for state approval is alignment with the state's content standards. In the summer of 2002, I examined science and social studies textbooks approved for adoption by the California Department of Education. I discovered many instances of superficial or otherwise inadequate development of standards in the approved texts that I reviewed. The most egregious shortcoming was the extensive use of end-of-chapter exercises and assessments such as word searches, labeling, and word-matching activities that required simple knowledge recall skills. All too often the expectations of exercises and assessments included in the approved texts fell far short of the rigorous expectations of California's state standards.

Another problem is the difference between the scope and sequence of the state standards and the scope and sequence of textbooks. When teachers follow a textbook chapter by chapter, they rarely finish the last two or three chapters by the end of the academic year. More important, they may not have finished substantial portions of the text by April or May when the state administers high-stakes exams. Although nationally marketed textbooks may include many topics of a given state's standards, they do not serve well as pacing guides for covering the standards of any one state before the administration of high-stakes tests.

Textbooks do not raise expectations for student learning; teachers do. In her evaluation of mathematics standards implementation in Missouri, Bay (2000) concludes that "a [standards-aligned] text-book, while supportive, is not sufficient to enable teachers to change their practices" (p. 3). Teachers should read and understand their state's standards and adjust their teaching and expectations accordingly. Textbook adoption cannot replace this all-important process.

Offering Professional Development Programs

State authorities and most research reports and policy studies on standards implementation recommend professional development as the most reliable method for changing instruction to achieve the standards. In California, the state department of education recom-mends that teachers receive professional development in the content of the state standards, frameworks, and state-approved curriculum materials. Unfortunately, research that Howard Kimmel of the New Jersey Institute of Technology and I conducted in New Jersey (O'Shea & Kimmel, 2003) raises questions about the value of professional development for standards implementation when it does not include standards-based lesson planning skills.

From 1998 to 2000, two urban school districts in New Jersey trained teachers to use curriculum activities aligned with the stan-dards. Teachers in the districts learned to teach with science activi-ties that were recommended in the state science framework. The logic of this training strategy is straightforward: If teachers learn and prac-tice activities that include the skills and content of the standards, then students will meet the standards as they perform the activities. Unfortunately, the study revealed that many teachers accepted stu-dents' work that did not meet the standards.

Almost all of the elementary school teachers in the two districts learned and practiced the new science activities. Twenty-five of the teachers volunteered to submit lesson plans that (1) referenced an appropriate New Jersey science standard and (2) included one of the activities taught in professional development sessions. After conducting the lessons, the teachers evaluated their students' work to see whether the selected science standard had been met. We asked teachers to identify the evidence of standards achievement by writing comments on copies of their students' work. Our analysis of the lesson plans, student work samples, and commentary about the student products revealed that most of the work did not meet the standards.

The New Jersey project, and similar research conducted in Oregon (Tell, Bodone, & Addie, 2000), suggests that teacher collaboration about the content and activities of lesson plans is an important component of professional development programs for standards achievement. Lesson and unit plans are valuable tools for instructional improvement in standards-based schools. When teachers write lesson plans with objectives that are taken from the standards, they focus their teaching efforts on student achievement of the standards. Although teachers need to know the content and skills of standards and frameworks, they also need to know how to set expectations and design learning experiences so that students demonstrate achievement of the standards.

Figure 2.1 (on p. 20) provides an overview of popular strategies for implementing standards and their relative merits. Chapter 4 will describe how such strategies, which fail when applied in isolation, can work well in combination with one another as a support system for standards achievement.

If standards alignment, textbook adoption, and conventional forms of professional development have already been used and students are not meeting the expectations of state and federal accountability measures, how should a school district move forward in addressing the challenge of the standards? To answer this question effectively, we must examine the singular shortcoming in these approaches, which centers on the role of the teacher in a standards-based system.

The Missing Component for Standards Achievement

The current state of standards and teaching in the United States resembles the "black box" model that scientists use to study unknown phenomena (see Figure 2.2 on p. 21). In this model, identifiable inputs and outputs of a system can be seen and described, but the process that gives rise to the outputs is the least understood part of the system.

FIGURE 2.1

Common Strategies for Implementing Standards

Strategy	Centrality to Teacher Role	Effectiveness
Align the school district curriculum with the content of the standards.	Distant from daily teaching but a very popular practice	Alignment may increase likelihood that topics are covered but does not address the need to change teachers' expectations.
Ask teachers to insert standards in lesson plans.	Central but a superficial action unlikely to affect teaching	Writing a standard in a plan does not translate into changed expectations.
Adopt texts that are aligned with the standards.	Central because use of a good text by teachers increases the likelihood of covering the standards	Textbook exercises and activities often fall below the expectations of state standards.
Ask teachers to closely examine the content of the standards and frameworks.	Central and an important exercise required for changing teaching practices	Knowledge of content in standards does not ensure changes in teaching.
Ask teachers to practice activities in the standards-aligned curriculum.	Central if teachers include activities in their teaching	Performance of activities does not mean expectations for students' work will meet the standards.
Time student achievement of the standards using a curriculum pacing guide.	Central because it focuses teaching on coverage of critical standards	Benchmark testing can ensure that standards are covered but does not affect quality of teaching.
Examine results of state standards tests to identify students who have performed poorly.	Distant from daily teaching	Knowledge of students' past performance does not change teaching.
Provide model unit and lesson plans that can serve as examples for teachers.	Central if used in classrooms	Examples may not affect other lessons or teachers' expectations for the quality of students' work.

FIGURE 2.2

Standards-Based Teaching as a "Black Box" Problem

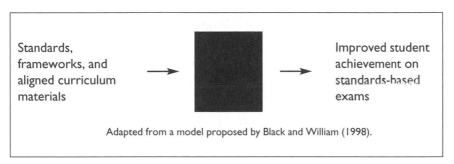

| Standards, frameworks, and aligned curriculum materials | → ■ → | Improved student achievement on standards-based exams |

Adapted from a model proposed by Black and William (1998).

So it is with standards-based teaching and learning. In almost every state, there are several identifiable state-sponsored "inputs" to the standards-based educational system:

• lists of standards, often accompanied by performance indicators and other elaborating statements, that describe the knowledge and skills to be acquired by students

• frameworks that provide information and resources to support the teaching of each standard, including teaching tips, suggested curriculum materials, and vignettes of teaching episodes

• test blueprints and state-released test items with information about standards-based exams used to assess student achievement of the standards

Curriculum alignment, pacing guides, and other capacity-building activities are also inputs in the evolving standards-based systems. Although helpful, they have no direct effect on the teaching and learning that take place in classrooms.

The "outputs" of the system capture the attention of education professionals and the public because they include the results on high-stakes tests that students take in the spring of each year. Also included are the consequences that befall underperforming schools that fail to make adequate yearly progress as prescribed by No Child Left Behind. In some states, students have been denied the right to graduate until they have passed a standards-based high school exit exam. Principals have lost their jobs when students' test scores have failed to improve.

Teachers find themselves caught in the middle between the standards resources, capacity-building exercises, and high-stakes tests. Some general recommendations have been given to teachers regarding their role in the standards system (e.g., use a standards-based curriculum and evaluate students' work more closely), but these recommendations are too vague to be of much use. Teachers want specific guidelines—often referred to as a *mechanism* or *theory of action*—for producing standards-based units and lessons that will result in standards-meeting work.

Nave, Miech, and Mosteller (2000), writing in the *Phi Delta Kappan,* address the need for a theory of action for standards implementation: "What mechanisms actually link the act of raising standards with improved student achievement?"(p. 128). The authors postulate that "if we had a sufficiently detailed theory of action that explained how standards could influence student achievement, then evaluation could focus closely on this hypothesized causal chain, with its particular expectations and assumptions, to see what happens when the new standards are put into practice" (p. 129). Teachers would benefit from a detailed theory of action as they plan standards-based instruction.

In California, underperforming schools receive extra funds to improve their achievement of the standards. Conditions accompany these extra funds. One important condition requires that teachers in the underperforming schools be given additional time to plan their work collaboratively. Unfortunately, teachers have not received a set of directions to follow, or a protocol to use during their extra planning time, that would help them turn the standards documents into standards-meeting lessons.

The need to provide teachers with a planning protocol was also revealed in a study of a large school district as it struggled with the standards. Ogawa, Sandholtz, Martinez-Flores, and Scribner (2003) conducted an in-depth study of a California school district's effort to install a standards-based educational system. In their report, they describe the essential elements of a rational system for educational improvement:

- Set specific goals (students achieve the standards).
- Adopt or develop an instructional technology for attaining the goals.
- Provide staff with training in the technology.
- Supervise employees to ensure execution of the technology.
- Assess the extent to which the goal is attained.
- Employ feedback to adjust operations. (pp. 162–163)

The school district developed critical standards for student achievement and aligned the curriculum with the standards. When it came time to tell teachers what they should do with the standards, the district leadership did not provide useful guidelines for teachers to use in the planning process. Simply stated, the district failed to provide a clear instructional technology for teachers to use during their lesson planning time.

The Search for a Standards-Meeting Protocol

By 1999, Kimmel and I recognized that a mechanism or protocol for standards-based instructional planning was the missing component in the comprehensive standards reform movement in the United States. Our review of the existing research literature revealed some promising initiatives that set the foundation for a theory of action, which developed into the Standards Achievement Planning Cycle (SAPC).

The Functional Standards of the New Standards Project

Our search for a planning protocol led us to the work of Resnick and Nolan (1995), who describe the functional components of standards-based systems that teachers can use to plan better lessons and raise expectations to meet the standards.[1] The first of these components, descriptions of content and skills expected of students, is readily available to teachers in the standards and frameworks of most states. Unfortunately, the other components either are found in obscure resources or are not developed at all. These valuable but difficult-to-find resources include

• descriptions of student performances that meet the expectations of the content statements

• "good enough" criteria that can be used to evaluate samples of students' work

• benchmark examples of students' work

• commentary on the benchmarks

Despite their apparent value, current editions of the standards, frameworks, and aligned curriculum resources fail to provide the resources described by Resnick and Nolan nearly 10 years ago. Content statements are usually provided, but performance descriptions with "good enough" criteria are missing. Kimmel and I saw Resnick and Nolan's components as essential tools that teachers need to meet the expectations of rigorous standards. Yet they are not sufficient for teachers who must work with different kinds of standards and frameworks to craft standards-meeting lessons.

The Japanese Lesson Study Model

Another initiative with the potential to help students meet standards is known as Japanese Lesson Study (Lewis & Tsuchida, 1998). This protocol, made widely known through the Third International Math and Science Study, is gaining popularity across the United States.

Teachers from California to New Jersey are adapting Japanese Lesson Study to conditions of teaching and learning in U.S. schools, and the National Science Foundation currently supports some of these efforts. This planning and lesson analysis protocol typically consists of three sequential activities. First, teachers collaborate in the planning of a lesson, pursuing a common goal of learning that they hope their students will achieve. Next, a small group teaches the resulting lesson while other teachers perform action research on the lesson as it is taught. Finally, researchers and observers disclose their findings in a follow-up session, identifying the lesson's successful elements. Kimmel and I found Japanese Lesson Study to be a promising cycle of teacher collaboration that leads to a supportive environment for standards-based lesson planning.

The Looking at Student Work Process

In our search, Kimmel and I reviewed another promising project that can link the standards to classroom assessment of student achievement. Teachers and university scholars are developing this initiative in several parts of the United States, and it takes on slightly different forms in its various locations of implementation. Generally, the process is called Looking at Student Work.

Looking at Student Work is gaining interest among educational reformers.[2] Teachers who participate in this activity bring students' work to team meetings. They follow certain guidelines and respond to prepared questions and prompts that lead them through an analysis of the work samples to gain deeper understanding about their students' comprehension of lessons. When teachers evaluate students' work and recognize shortcomings in learning, they adjust their teaching accordingly. Howard Kimmel and I knew that this process should be an essential component of an effective standards-achieving protocol.

The Emergence of the Standards Achievement Planning Cycle

Thanks to funding from the National Science Foundation, Kimmel and I were able to work closely with teachers and examine their activities in instructional planning and student work evaluation as state content standards were emerging in New Jersey from 1998 through 2002. As a result of this clinical work in New Jersey and California and our research into the promising initiatives described above, the SAPC began to emerge. This new protocol, which is fully presented in Chapter 3, is based on three essential premises or core beliefs. These premises reflect effective schools research and policy research involving standards implementation.

First, we believe that teaching is a planned activity. Well-developed plans are the instruments of successful teaching and student learning. Without plans, teachers lose sight of their targets for student learning and fall back on less important measures of teaching success such as students' enjoyment of lessons and good behavior. Although enjoyment of lessons is certainly desirable, only effective planning leads to well-described instructional targets for standards-meeting work.

Second, we presume good faith on the part of state authorities and test development companies that prepare high-stakes standards tests. State standards tests must include only information found in the standards, frameworks, and related state resources. Students who can fully meet the learning expectations described in state standards documents should score well on state exams. "Teaching to the test" should be unnecessary if the state exam items are properly taken from the standards. In a standards-based lesson planning system, the target of instruction should be the content and skills of the standards, along with additional curriculum content that fully prepares young people for life's experiences. Anticipated test questions should not become the targets of instruction.

Finally, we believe that teachers need to be deeply immersed in the process of setting learning expectations for their own students. Students will produce standards-meeting work when their teachers set expectations for their learning. Externally prepared guides and curriculum resources can be helpful, but only teachers can make the planning decisions that will result in improved student learning.

The SAPC includes activities on planning lessons, teaching, and evaluating students' work. Teachers develop these components while working collaboratively in functional units such as grade-level teams or secondary school departments. All organizational changes and activities in the curriculum management model for standards achievement are dedicated to supporting the successful work of collaborative teams as they implement the SAPC.

Although several important outcomes result from the SAPC, none is more important than the collaborative planning of a truly standards-based lesson. These lessons are not to be confused with "standards-aligned" lessons that ensure only topical coverage of a selected standard. The lessons that emerge from the Planning Cycle envision student performances and products that meet or exceed the expectations of the standards. Teachers structure their lessons to achieve these outcomes.

The Elements of a Standards-Based Lesson

We can understand the distinctive characteristics of a standards-based lesson by comparing an example of such a lesson with a conventional lesson plan. Figure 2.3 shows a conventional 3rd

FIGURE 2.3

Typical Lesson Plan for 3rd Grade Social Studies

Topic: The effects of pioneer settlement on communities over time

Rationale: Students should understand the heritage and legacy of events brought about by early settlers in the new world. They should appreciate the lasting heritage that they see reflected in local place names and the artifacts of early settlement.

Objectives: Students will learn about important economic activities of early settlers. They will learn how early settlers survived and how they made a living. Students will know how these early economies changed over time.

These objectives will serve no use in curriculum management. They do not tell us what students are expected to do as an outcome of the lesson. The teacher cannot use them to evaluate students' work.

Materials: Text reading: pp. 120–123 describing the process of clearing the land for settlement and elements of everyday pioneer life

Activities: Students will be expected to read the passage as homework the night before. During class, students will respond to questions about the reading assignment, identifying tools used by settlers, describing how they made a living and to whom they sold goods, and explaining how they made things or gathered items for sale. Students will then complete answers to questions on a worksheet derived from a passage in their textbook.

Assessment: Completed worksheets will be evaluated for accuracy. Students will be expected to describe tools used by settlers, crops grown, and game hunted. They must identify specific items of merchandise sold to city dwellers.

grade social studies lesson plan about pioneer communities. Typical elements of a conventional plan are listed, including the topic, a rationale for the lesson, the objectives, the materials to be used, the activities that will unfold in the classroom, and a method for evaluating student learning. In this example, the objectives provide information about the topic of the lesson, describing what students are to learn in relation to the selected topic. The objectives do not describe the ultimate products or observable behaviors students will display to demonstrate achievement of a standard.

In many schools, a conventional plan is converted into a "standards-based" plan by simply adding a standard matched to the lesson topic. Figure 2.4 consists of the conventional plan of Figure 2.3 after it has been supposedly "upgraded" to a standards-based plan by adding a standard. The content standard has been inserted between the rationale and the objectives. Unfortunately, this mere transcription of a standard from a state document to a lesson plan will not make the lesson truly standards-based because it does not change expectations for student learning.

From Figure 2.4 we can see that the content of the selected standard is quite similar to the topic of our conventional lesson. This reflects the current concern for aligning classroom instruction with the standards. Yet the alignment of a lesson topic with a standard does not guarantee that students will achieve the learning expectations of the standard. It only ensures that the topic of the standard will be covered.

In contrast, Figure 2.5 (on p. 30) presents a truly standards-based lesson that results from following the SAPC protocol. Explicit student learning outcomes appear in the objectives. The outcomes describe behaviors or products that meet the expectations of the standard. The outcomes meet the standards because teachers formulate them directly from the content statements in the standards and frameworks. After teachers write objectives from the standards and frameworks, they select and sequence curriculum resources and instructional activities to elicit the desired performances described in the objectives.

FIGURE 2.4

Lesson Plan for 3rd Grade Social Studies with Standards Statement

Topic: The effects of pioneer settlement on communities over time

Rationale: Students should understand the heritage and legacy of events
                   brought about by early settlers in the new world. They
                   should appreciate the lasting heritage that they see reflected
                   in local place names and the artifacts of early settlement.

**Content
Standard:**   History–Social Science
                   3.3 Students draw from historical and community resources
                       to organize the sequence of local historical events and
                       describe how each period of settlement left its mark on
                       the land.
                       2. Describe the economies established by settlers and
                          their influence on the present-day economy, with
                          emphasis on the importance of private property and
                          entrepreneurship.[3]

This standard was taken from the state standards or frameworks.

Objectives: Students will learn about important economic activities of
                   early settlers. They will learn how early settlers survived and
                   how they made a living. Students will know how these early
                   economies changed over time.

*Although the selected standard has the same topic as the objectives,
this simple alignment does not make the lesson
a more powerful tool for teaching.*

Materials: Text reading: pp. 120–123 describing the process of clearing
                   the land for settlement and elements of everyday pioneer life

Activities: Students will be expected to read the passage as homework
                   the night before. During class, students will respond to ques-
                   tions about the reading assignment, identifying tools used by
                   settlers, describing how they made a living and to whom they
                   sold goods, and explaining how they made things or gathered
                   items for sale. Students will then complete answers to ques-
                   tions on a worksheet derived from a passage in their textbook.

Assessment: Completed worksheets will be evaluated for accuracy.
                   Students will be expected to describe tools used by settlers,
                   crops grown, and game hunted. They must identify specific
                   items of merchandise sold to city dwellers.

FIGURE 2.5

Standards-Based Lesson Plan for 3rd Grade Social Studies

Topic: The effects of pioneer settlement on communities over time

Rationale: Students should understand the heritage and legacy of events brought about by early settlers in the new world. They should appreciate the lasting heritage that they see reflected in local place names and the artifacts of early settlement.

Content Standard: History–Social Science

3.3 Students draw from historical and community resources to organize the sequence of local historical events and describe how each period of settlement left its mark on the land.

    2. Describe the economies established by settlers and their influence on the present-day economy, with emphasis on the importance of private property and entrepreneurship.[4]

Learning expectations for this standard appear in the state frameworks. They have been translated into outcomes-based language in the new lesson objectives listed below.

Objectives:
- Students *will write* the names of Native American groups that lived within the school district boundaries and *state* three economic activities or products that sustained their daily life. They *will give* reasons why these products were made.
- Students *will place* specific examples of street names, place names, and other legacies of Native Americans on a district map provided by the teacher. Students *will state* why the names are still used.
- Students *will prepare* a time line showing the duration of Native Americans in this area and the arrival of pioneers.
- Students *will list* the agricultural and hunting products used by settlers for trade with Native Americans. They also *will identify* products sold at market in villages and emerging cities.

The objectives include descriptions of student products or behaviors that should result from teaching. These objectives will be the basis for evaluating students' work.

FIGURE 2.5 (continued)

Materials:	• Text reading: pp. 120–123 describing the process of clearing the land for settlement and elements of everyday pioneer life • Regional map showing the school district boundaries
Activities:	Students will be expected to read the passage as homework the night before. They will construct a time line with a narrative under each critical event marking the period of occupation by Native Americans. Students will include the arrival of pioneers and indicate agricultural and hunting products on the time line. Students will locate Native American place names on a map of the district. During class, students will respond to questions about the reading assignment, identifying tools used by settlers, describing how they made a living and to whom they sold goods, and explaining how they made things or gathered items for sale. Students will then complete answers to questions on a worksheet derived from a passage in their textbook.

These activities are recommended in the frameworks. They have been modified and organized by the teacher to elicit the outcomes in the objectives.

Assessment:	At the end of class, students will write a paragraph describing what they would like to grow or make as a son or a daughter of a pioneer family. They will state where the raw materials for their products came from and identify customers for their products. In addition, maps will be evaluated for accurate placement of street names and place names. The time lines will be evaluated for accurate identification of the time when pioneers arrived and the products that were made in various time periods.

A truly standards-based lesson can be used to answer the following questions that arise in the process of managing the curriculum for standards achievement:

• Are teachers setting expectations for student learning that are based on the standards?

• Are students providing work that meets or exceeds the standards?

• Do our teachers know the content of the standards?

These questions cannot be answered by the conventional lesson plan provided in Figure 2.3 or by a lesson that simply includes the text of a standard, as seen in Figure 2.4. The standards-based lesson in Figure 2.5, however, does answer all these important questions. The effectiveness of the lesson can be seen in the actions of the students. Most important, the lesson plan in Figure 2.5 can be used to evaluate students' work in comparison with the learning expectations of the standards.

How the Planning Cycle Results in Standards Achievement

There is nothing truly original about the SAPC. It is a synthesis of ideas associated with outcomes-based education, Japanese Lesson Study, Resnick and Nolan's functional standards, Looking at Student Work, and the use of state standards as instructional targets. In the SAPC, learning outcomes written from standards and frameworks form the instructional targets of standards-based lesson plans. The lesson objectives consist of observable skills or products that students will demonstrate and teachers can evaluate. Standards were originally intended for this role in instructional planning. Their use as guides to align or correlate curriculum is an important but secondary purpose.

The SAPC is a five-step process of collaborative decision making that helps teachers produce standards-meeting lessons. When teachers conduct the SAPC, they focus their attention on the specific elements of content standards that will be achieved during a lesson. These steps unfold in a sequence of actions described below and explained in greater detail in the next chapter.

Step 1: Identifying Standards

When teachers use textbooks and activities as the primary resources to plan lessons, they are not focusing on the content that students must know for high-stakes tests. Textbooks and activities are resources that help students meet the objectives of a standards-based lesson, but they should not be used to identify the targets of instruction. Only the state standards, frameworks that include the standards, and related state resources such as test blueprints are appropriate for this function.

We need to keep in mind that state standards and frameworks are powerful instruments in our current reform agenda. Although they were originally intended to identify the essential topics and skills to be learned by students, they have become the core state curriculum that all students are expected to learn. The achievement of state standards will result in adequate yearly progress under the federal No Child Left Behind Act. In the SAPC, teachers use state standards documents to identify the essential knowledge and skills to be included in their lessons.

Step 2: Analyzing Standards

Working in groups, teachers examine standards and frameworks to identify the essential content that students must learn. Although a seemingly simple task, the complex nature of standards, frameworks, and related state standards documents makes the process of identifying learning expectations a challenging experience. Frameworks and standards are rarely organized as instructional planning tools. The information that teachers need for lesson planning may be commingled with tips for teaching, suggestions for finding resources, policy statements involving the subject matter to be taught, and vignettes of teaching episodes. Teachers must identify the content statements in the standards and frameworks that describe what students are to know or be able to do. Teachers must focus on these statements for their lessons and then transform them into useful descriptions of student performances in the next stage of the SAPC.

Step 3: Describing Student Performances

The preparation of student performance descriptions from content statements is the most challenging step of the SAPC. Knowledge and skill statements contained in frameworks and standards are the source material for these descriptions. Teachers can use them to write clear, explicit descriptions of products and behaviors that they expect from students. These descriptions serve two purposes. First, they express the objectives, or instructional targets, for the teacher. They guide the teacher's efforts toward the achievement of specific standards. Second, they serve as evaluation tools for daily teaching. Performance descriptions can be used to evaluate students' work in comparison with the expectations of the standards.

The translation of content statements from standards documents into useful student learning outcomes is a more difficult task if standards are written as vague, overly broad statements. When teachers are beset with this challenge, the old adage applies: Two minds are better than one. Teachers working collaboratively to arrive at a professional judgment are better able to overcome the deficiencies in vaguely written standards and create performance descriptions that will result in standards-meeting work.

Step 4: Selecting Learning Activities

After teachers have decided what their students will do or produce to meet the standards selected for the lesson, they can judge the adequacy of the textbook or other resources to achieve the desired learning outcomes. Often, teachers may decide that their textbooks need to be supplemented with other resources in order for students to demonstrate the expected skills and knowledge included in their lesson plans. If teachers rely on a text or other commercial resource to plan lessons, they may never notice the text's deficiencies in eliciting student skills and knowledge described in the standards.

Planning lesson activities and presenting them to students in a coherent order comprise the second most challenging task in standards-based teaching. It is during this process that teachers demonstrate their special skills as educators. To perform this function effectively, the teacher must

• know the subject matter of the standards and frameworks;

• anticipate student difficulties in demonstrating the behaviors or producing the work that will meet the expectations of the standards;

• locate instructional resources beyond the textbook, including activities, appropriate media, and formative assessment tasks; and

• sequence activities into a coherent, developmental experience for students that will result in the achievement of lesson objectives.

Again, teachers are more likely to exercise this creative skill when they work collaboratively to review curriculum materials, choose among alternative resources, and decide on the best sequence of activities. Once these decisions are made, the lesson plan is complete. The teachers can organize their classrooms, gather materials, and teach the lesson to achieve the desired outcomes.

Step 5: Evaluating Students' Work

If teachers are successful in teaching the standards-based lesson that they planned in Steps 1 through 4, their students will meet the expectations of the selected standards. The evidence of this achievement should be found in students' work collected during or after the lesson. In the last step of the SAPC, teachers compare student work samples with the descriptions of student performances in the lesson's objectives. If the performance descriptions are written carefully and provide vivid depictions of the work expected from students, the descriptions will serve as assessment tools in evaluating students' work. Teachers sit together to examine their students' work and determine whether it includes the expected properties of a standards-meeting performance.

Enabling Conditions for the Planning Cycle

Schools can be organized to support teachers as they work in teams to follow the various steps of the SAPC. Fortunately, many of the strategies for standards implementation in use by school districts today can be combined to form a coherent system of support services and resources that help teachers plan standards-based lessons. Figure 2.6 (on p. 36) describes the enabling conditions, in chronological order, that a district can establish to support teachers in their lesson planning and work evaluation activities. Each enabling condition is discussed briefly in the following sections; Chapter 4 provides a more complete description of all seven components of the enabling system.

FIGURE 2.6

Enabling Conditions for Meeting the Standards

1. Get standards documents into the hands of teachers; ensure that they learn the structure and content of the standards and frameworks.

2. Identify the critical standards to be achieved in each grade level and in each core subject; include them in the district's curriculum guides.
   • Recognize that identifying standards and updating curriculum guides is an ongoing process.
   • Monitor state testing policy and procedures to identify standards that are tested.

3. Supplement the curriculum guide with pacing information.
   • Explicitly state which standards will be achieved, in what order, and when they will be achieved during the academic year.
   • Include respected teachers in the development of the pacing guidelines.

4. Use the curriculum guides to select standards-aligned texts, with attention to
   • rate and pace of standards coverage,
   • alignment at each grade level for core subjects,
   • academic vocabulary of standards and frameworks, and
   • quality of activities to elicit expected student outcomes.

5. Modify school schedules to include collaboration time for lesson planning and student work evaluation.

6. Ask lead teachers and the assessment coordinator to develop a program for benchmark testing.

7. Conduct political advocacy for the standards and set the stage for professional development.

Providing Copies of Essential Standards Documents

Elementary and secondary school teachers need different sets of resources to meet their obligations with the standards. Elementary school teachers need copies of the standards, frameworks, and related state standards documents for each of the core subjects. Secondary school teachers need the K–12 resources for reading, mathematics, and their subject area. They also must be familiar with the standards for the lower grades because the standards describe the foundation that each student should bring into the secondary school classroom. In addition, all teachers must know the organizational structure and content of the state standards documents in each of the core areas at the elementary level and in the teaching assignment at the secondary level.

Updating the District's Curriculum Guides

Aligning a district's curriculum with the knowledge and skills of the standards is the most frequent response to the standards, as discussed at the beginning of the chapter. However, this alignment activity is a prerequisite to standards-based teaching, not an end in itself. Lead teachers and curriculum coordinators identify the critical standards to be achieved in core subjects at each grade level. Model lesson plans and activities, exemplary student work, and sample test items can be included in the curriculum guides only after standards have been assigned to each grade level and to each subject in the school curriculum.

Developing Standards Pacing Information

Through curriculum mapping, the district determines the subjects and grade levels in which critical standards are to be achieved during the academic year. Curriculum pacing takes the process a step further, determining the sequence and the rate at which standards should be achieved. The pacing information is essential because it helps ensure that students will be prepared for annual high-stakes tests.

Choosing Texts After Curriculum Mapping

Finding the best textbooks for standards-based teaching and learning is possible only after the district has determined the grade levels and sequence in which critical standards are to be taught. The district's standards pacing guidelines are essential resources for the selection of textbooks.

Teachers will find a text more useful if it contains activities and exercises that meet the expectations of the standards and frameworks. Furthermore, the readability of the resources should match the rigorous academic vocabulary found in the standards and frameworks. High-quality texts that are well aligned with the pacing guidelines are essential tools for planning standards-meeting lessons.

The Myth of the Standards-Aligned Textbook

Textbook publishers know that each state has its own content standards. The problem for publishers is providing an answer to the question "Is your textbook aligned to our state's standards?" Clearly, the publisher wants to say yes. But how can this goal be accomplished for every state, given that it is economically unfeasible to produce an original textbook for each state's standards? Publishing companies address this problem by supplementing the text in those states that have substantial markets, including Texas and California.

For smaller states, textbook publishers provide a standards correlation matrix, showing where each standard is addressed in the text. In a secondary school subject such as chemistry or U.S. history, this poses little difficulty. In the elementary grades, however, problems begin to emerge. In reviewing state-adopted social studies and science texts for elementary grades in California, I found a number of problems:

- The content of many state standards is covered within a textbook series, but not at the grade level for which the standard was written.

- The content for a given set of grade-level materials used by a teacher is matched to state standards for a different grade level.

- Social studies content described in the state framework is not included in the nationally produced textbooks.

Adjusting the School Schedule to Support Planning

If curriculum alignment is a district's most common response to the standards, modification of the daily teaching schedule to accommodate collaborative lesson planning may be the least frequent response. The SAPC identifies specific activities to be performed during collaborative planning sessions, and administrators should install a curriculum management system that oversees the productivity of these sessions. Schools clearly need to allocate more time for standards-based planning. When adjustments in the school schedule are made, opportunities for instructional improvement will follow.

Creating a Benchmark-Testing Program

School leaders will want to know that standards achievement is progressing smoothly from classroom to classroom and from school to school across the district. Moreover, teachers will want confirming information that their students have truly met the standards selected for their lessons. Although evaluation of students' work during the SAPC provides a valuable source of information about standards achievement, a series of benchmark tests will determine if students are retaining the skills and knowledge of the standards. Benchmark tests will also prepare students for the high-stakes state tests usually administered in the spring. Benchmark tests can be administered periodically through the year and are an essential component of the districtwide assessment system.

Advocating for Standards Achievement

The procurement of resources and the adjustment of school schedules to facilitate collaborative lesson planning will not yield desired results unless teachers, students, parents, and community members believe in standards achievement as an important goal for all students. Unfortunately, there is a great deal of hostility to standards as an element of the No Child Left Behind Act. School leaders will need an effective communications program to address resistance to the standards and to promote their inherent value for student learning. As preparations are made to install the SAPC, leaders should discuss the importance of the standards with school district constituents.

In most settings, at least one of the enabling conditions cited in Figure 2.6 is already in place. Perhaps the curriculum is aligned or texts have been adopted. The important next step is installing the remaining enabling conditions and organizing them into a coherent system of supporting resources and services. When installed, these resources establish the foundation of standards-based planning and teaching. After the enabling conditions are set in place, district leaders need to direct their attention to the new roles and responsibilities that the SAPC creates.

Sustaining Conditions for the Planning Cycle

The SAPC will be sustained by teachers if it is supported by a well-conceived assessment system. The system should include several levels of evaluation activity, beginning with classroom-based assessments, benchmark testing, and complete analysis of district results on state standards tests.

Using Classroom-Based Assessments

During SAPC training, teachers will learn to use the standards-based lesson objective as the first-level assessment tool for daily classroom teaching. When lesson objectives are written as student outcomes, they become tools that teachers can use to quickly evaluate their students' work.

Introducing Benchmark Tests

When standards have been properly mapped and the district curriculum is fully aligned with the standards, benchmark testing can be introduced to provide ongoing measurement of standards achievement. Benchmark testing supports and validates assessment of student achievement while teachers undertake the new planning and teaching procedures of the SAPC. It shows teachers whether their students are meeting the standards well before the state test is administered, and it helps planning teams identify areas of curriculum weakness before students encounter state tests.

Benchmark testing also enables the curriculum management team to determine how schools and teachers are doing as they lead students to standards achievement through the SAPC. Benchmark tests, typically only 30 or 40 minutes long, are administered three or four times a year. Teachers prepare test items from frameworks and standards, and they structure the distribution of test items by type to resemble the distribution seen on state tests. Through such quick feedback, teachers can adjust their teaching to ensure student readiness for high-stakes tests, usually administered in the spring. The testing program can assure school leaders that students are ready for the state tests.

Analyzing Test Results

Finally, school leaders can analyze state test results to improve instruction. District assessment coordinators use software to disaggregate state test results to meet No Child Left Behind reporting requirements. This kind of analysis can be used to target standards where student underperformance is a problem or to identify groups of students who may need extra assistance. Leaders can also analyze the benchmark test results to achieve similar purposes. Conducting a thorough analysis of student performance through both forms of assessment confirms the conclusions reached by evaluating students' work as part of the SAPC.

Classroom assessments, benchmark testing, and analysis of state test results form a comprehensive assessment system to measure standards achievement. Some districts will use other standardized tests to measure student achievement. Although these exams can compare local student performances with student performances in other districts, they do not assess how well students are progressing toward mastery of the state standards.

**Standards-Based Tests and Standardized Tests:
Similar Names but Different Purposes**

Newspaper articles and radio reports continue to describe student achievement results on state tests. Often, these reports fail to state whether the exam in question is a criterion-referenced standards-based test or a norm-referenced standardized test, commonly used to measure student performance prior to widespread adoption of state standards. *Norm-referenced standardized tests* rely on test questions of varied difficulty to identify low- and high-performing students. The purpose of these tests is to compare the performance of a student or group of students with the performance of a population of other students, typically a state or national population. Although they are effective in comparing one student's skills or knowledge with that of other students, they serve no purpose in measuring student achievement of the content of the standards.

In contrast, *criterion-referenced standards-based tests,* now used by many states, measure the performance of a student or a group of students in relation to the skills and knowledge of state standards and frameworks. These exams evaluate student achievement against an identified body of knowledge, not a comparable group of students. The media rarely make this distinction known to the public when reporting state test results.

Providing District Support

With the SAPC in place, district administrators have new responsibilities, for teachers will be able to make effective use of the protocol only if they are given the curriculum resources, time, and professional support to do the job well. Moreover, they will persist with the SAPC only if they believe that their efforts will make a positive difference for their students and will be supported by the administration.

Broad-based community support for the SAPC and the curriculum management system is needed because these methods call for changes in the roles and responsibilities of teachers and administrators. Funds for professional development are required. Community members must be persuaded that time spent by teachers conducting the SAPC is time well spent. District leaders will be able to persuade community members of the need for change if they can readily describe the elements of the curriculum management system and the SAPC.

Instructional planning with the SAPC calls for the exercise of professional judgment, and opportunities for error exist in each step of the process. Thus, teachers need support and assistance in making decisions as they plan instruction and evaluate students' work. If school districts employ curriculum coordinators in various disciplines, the coordinators can provide technical assistance for teachers as they implement the SAPC. If curriculum coordinators are not available, then lead teachers may need to fulfill this role in the curriculum management process.

Evaluating Standards Achievement in Your School

As a comprehensive response to the state standards environment in California, the La Senda School District followed the SAPC protocol for lesson planning and student work evaluation. They put in place the enabling conditions and a curriculum management system necessary for success with the SAPC.

School districts across the country have responded in different ways to their standards mandate. Some have made impressive progress in developing a coherent system that meets state standards.

School leaders may want to use the checklist in Figure 2.7 to assess their progress in helping students achieve the standards.

FIGURE 2.7

Checklist of Local Standards Implementation Efforts

State content standards

_____ are familiar to some teachers but dismissed by many others.

_____ are met through curriculum materials aligned to the standards.

_____ are understood by teachers and accepted by most of them.

_____ are prioritized locally for their relative importance.

_____ are used to write lesson objectives.

_____ are used to select curriculum resources.

_____ are the essential cornerstones of the district's curriculum guide, which is aligned to the scope and sequence of the standards.

The local curriculum

_____ has remained unchanged since state standards were adopted.

_____ is currently aligned with national standards but not state standards.

_____ has been thoroughly aligned with state standards.

_____ is paced to ensure timely achievement of critical state standards identified at the district level.

_____ is supported by a benchmark-testing system based on critical state standards.

Teachers

_____ are waiting for the standards movement to pass from the scene.

_____ are beginning to align their teaching with the topics and skills of the state standards.

_____ have been provided with the most recent editions of state standards.

_____ use frameworks (or similar state resources) and information about the state's high-stakes tests to plan instruction.

_____ work with standards selected by the district.

_____ follow curriculum pacing guides to ensure critical standards are achieved before state tests are administered.

_____ use supplemental planning time to meet with colleagues for standards-based planning and student work evaluation.

(continued)

FIGURE 2.7   (continued)

Principals

_____ cannot describe the district's strategy for standards achievement.

_____ are also waiting for the standards movement to fade away.

_____ use faculty meetings to support standards achievement by all students.

_____ look for evidence that standards are addressed in classrooms.

_____ look for evidence of standards achievement during the supervisory process.

_____ use the district's assessment system to focus teachers' efforts on standards achievement.

Problems with standards implementation are evident if a check mark has been placed before the first two items in any of the categories of the checklist. Check marks before the subsequent items in each category suggest that the district has made progress with standards achievement. Check marks before the final item in each category indicate that substantial progress in standards achievement is under way.

3

The Standards Achievement Planning Cycle

Chapter 2 introduced the Standards Achievement Planning Cycle (SAPC) as a theory of action or a series of steps that teachers can follow to translate the learning expectations of state standards into powerful lessons that focus on standards achievement. If the SAPC is successfully installed in a school, teachers can use it to achieve adequate yearly progress as required by the No Child Left Behind Act.

Teachers are most deeply immersed in their professional role when they make judgments and decisions that affect student learning. We might tend to believe that the important decisions are made during the actual process of instruction, but as we will see in this chapter, the SAPC guides judgments and decisions *before* instruction, when teachers collaboratively plan their lessons.

It is important to note that the SAPC is not a turnkey formula for translating state standards documents into standards achievement. On the contrary, the SAPC functions well only when educated teachers with curriculum expertise apply their imagination, creativity, and knowledge about resources to plan standards-meeting lessons for their students.

The Five Steps of the Planning Cycle

Let us return to Mariposa Elementary School, where 2nd grade teacher Mrs. Hernandez and two of her colleagues are involved in a lesson planning session. Mrs. Lewis, the principal, worked with administrative colleagues to provide all teachers at Mariposa with extensive planning time each Wednesday afternoon. As we join the teachers in their planning activities, we see that they have some essential resources with them: the state frameworks for science and reading/language arts, the district's science curriculum guide with standards pacing information, and locally adopted science curriculum materials purchased by the district.

In subsequent years, the teachers will have other resources to make their planning easier, including the lesson they are about to prepare, samples of exemplary work submitted by students in response to the lesson, and notes about the quality features in the students' work.

Step 1: Identify Standards to Be Addressed

The teachers begin their work by turning to the district's curriculum guide and pacing information. This resource provides teachers with the specific standards that should be covered, the order in which they should be developed, and most important, the standard, or portion of a standard, that should be addressed in the specific lesson they are planning. The curriculum pacing guidelines display the standards that Mrs. Hernandez and her colleagues should be teaching before the next benchmark test. The framework and text inform them of the depth and breadth of skills and content that students must know to meet the standard.

Through prior training, Mrs. Hernandez and her fellow teachers know the challenge before them: They must select a reasonable amount of knowledge for students to learn while maintaining the rate of standards achievement described in the pacing guidelines. It is possible to select either too many or too few standards. In the New Jersey study of standards-based lesson planning discussed in Chapter 2, for example, several participating teachers chose too many standards to convey in the lesson plans they submitted (O'Shea & Kimmel, 2003). Student work samples resulting from lesson plans with too many standards demonstrated superficial coverage of topics in each selected standard rather than high-quality, thoughtful work.

The tendency to select too many standards suggests that teachers sense the inherent conflict between needing to cover the standards in depth and maintaining a pace that will ensure student achievement of all essential material. For Mrs. Hernandez and her colleagues, another consideration is how to select science content, science process, and reading/language arts standards that can be developed concurrently within the same lesson without selecting too many standards in total.

The district's curriculum pacing information draws the teachers' attention to the 2nd grade science content standard sets and specific standards from the California science framework. In the framework, standard sets are numbered, and letters precede specific standards. The teachers focus on the second standard set for the life sciences and its first three standards:

> 2. Plants and animals have predictable life cycles. As a basis for understanding this concept:
>   a. *Students know* that organisms reproduce offspring of their own kind and that the offspring resemble their parents and one another.
>   b. *Students know* the sequential stages of life cycles are different for different animals, such as butterflies, frogs, and mice.
>   c. *Students know* many characteristics of an organism are inherited from the parents. Some characteristics are caused or influenced by the environment. (California Department of Education, 2003, p. 39)[1]

The Mariposa students have met the first standard of the standard set, and the teachers are ready to work with the second standard: "*Students know* the sequential stages of life cycles are different for different animals, such as butterflies, frogs, and mice."

Now that they have identified a specific science standard, Mrs. Hernandez and her colleagues prepare to review other standards. During professional development, they learned that science includes important content and process standards. The *process* standards convey the ways of learning and knowing in science (investigation and experimentation skills, for example); the *content* standards focus on science facts and principles. This understanding leads our teachers to find process standards to be achieved or practiced concurrently with content standards.

While reviewing the guide, they select the following process standard from the fourth standard set, investigation and experimentation:

> 4. Scientific progress is made by asking meaningful questions and conducting careful investigations. . . .
>   d. Students will write or draw descriptions of a sequence of steps, events, and observations. (California Department of Education, 2003, p. 44)[2]

The teachers know the content related to the life cycles of butterflies, frogs, and mice. They believe the selected process standard can be exercised and strengthened through activities that also develop the selected content standard.

The simultaneous teaching of process standards from language arts and mathematics with content and skills standards of social studies or science helps to achieve a large number of standards during the school year. In our example, Mrs. Hernandez's team decides to supplement the science standards with standards from language arts. Typically, teachers in the 2nd grade hope to develop language arts skills as a companion goal for a science lesson because they are held accountable for adequate yearly progress in language arts.

The three teachers turn to the language arts section of the curriculum pacing guide. The guide informs them that the following writing standard, taken from the *Reading/Language Arts Framework for California Public Schools,* should be met concurrently with their selected science standard:

> 2.1 Students write brief narratives based on their experiences:
>   a. Move through a logical sequence of events.
>   b. Describe the setting, characters, objects, and events in detail.
>   (California Department of Education, 1999, p. 78)[3]

At the conclusion of the first step of the SAPC, Mrs. Hernandez and her colleagues have selected a specific standard from a science content standard set, a science process standard, and two language arts standards. Their primary resource for this activity is the standards pacing information in the district's curriculum guide. The state content standards may include elaborating statements that help with this process. If the teachers perform this first task well— identifying standards to be addressed—they will have selected the proper amount of challenging material to keep their students progressing through the curriculum in anticipation of a later benchmark test.

Step 2: Analyze the Selected Standards and the Frameworks

The next step of the SAPC entails looking more closely at the selected standards and related narrative in the frameworks. The frameworks include the essential information and skills that students must master to perform well on the state's high-stakes tests. Continuing with our example, Mrs. Hernandez and her fellow teachers turn their attention to the contents of the science and reading/language arts frameworks that address the state's content standards.

The science framework is well organized as a reference tool for teachers. Content statements and other useful information can be found right under each standard. The teachers review the information under the standard they have chosen to work with:

> **b.** *Students know* **the sequential stages of life cycles are different for different animals, such as butterflies, frogs, and mice.**
>
> **The life cycles of some insects consist of egg, larval, pupal, and adult stages. Many organisms undergo molting processes during the larval stage or the adult stage. This phenomenon is typical of species that have tough external skeletons (e.g., grasshoppers, crabs).** Using mealworms (obtainable from many pet stores and kept in plastic containers with bran meal) is a good way for students to watch the life cycle of grain beetles over a period of a few weeks. The life cycles of these insects can be slowed down by placing the containers in the refrigerator at night and over weekends. Mealworms molt as they grow during their larval stages, and the casings can be easily recovered for study. **Frogs and many other amphibians also undergo a type of metamorphosis, but those changes unfold gradually. Mammals bear live young that resemble, to a great extent, their adult forms.** (California Department of Education, 2003, p. 39, emphasis added)[4]

This passage in the framework that relates to our selected standard includes different kinds of statements. Some statements provide suggestions for teaching methods. Other statements explain why certain ideas or principles are important for students to learn. The boldface sections identify the key content statements that

Mrs. Hernandez and her colleagues have chosen for their students to master. The remaining sentences in the passage are recommendations for teaching.

The boldface material contains the vocabulary, concepts, and some of the essential skills that students should know to meet the selected standards. Let's examine the first highlighted statement, the standard that the teachers selected for their lesson. If we focus on important subject-matter words in the standard, we find these highly challenging terms for 2nd grade students: *sequential, stages,* and *life cycles.* Although we may be confident that most 2nd grade students know the words *butterfly, frog,* or *mouse* when they see a picture of one of these animals, we cannot be equally confident that they will understand the words *sequence, sequential,* or *stages* or the important concept of life cycles. These terms will need to be experienced, conceptually developed, and retained by the students. They are not only the language of the frameworks and standards; they are the critical vocabulary and concepts most likely to appear in state standards tests.

When the teachers review the other highlighted sentences in the passage, they find the names of important insect stages, including *egg, larval, pupal,* and *adult.* What of the unnamed stages, such as *tadpole* for a frog? Mrs. Hernandez and her colleagues need to analyze the content statements to identify critical concepts that students must know. They also need to consider implied information that may not be specifically mentioned but is nevertheless important for children if they are to fully understand the concepts.

At this point, the 2nd grade teachers have extracted the important information from the framework for their science content standard. But what will they do with their selected science process standard and their language arts standards, also scheduled for development in the pacing guide? Typically, process standards involving the application of skills are best left for consideration during the next two stages of the SAPC: drafting student learning expectations and selecting learning activities. Often, opportunities to develop skills and investigative processes arise from the consideration of activities used to elicit content understanding.

How Do We Know the Statements That Will Be Tested?

Content statements can be found in two different kinds of narrative included in frameworks. The first of these are the standards. Most state frameworks also include descriptions of instructional activities and additional statements explaining the content of the standards. Do the state tests evaluate students' knowledge of content found only in standards? Will the additional detail and factual knowledge of the elaborating statements also appear on state standards tests? Put simply, how deeply into the frameworks must teachers search to find content likely to be tested on state exams?

In California, the released test items show that the state history and social science tests do not assess the content that appears in the extensive narrative sections outside the standards statements. Released test items are only derived from actual standards statements. By contrast, the state standards tests for science do include details in the explanatory narrative of the framework that is found outside the standards statements. The implications of this distinction are significant. California teachers can prepare their students for success with the state history and social science tests by writing lesson objectives from standards statements only. When California teachers conduct the SAPC in science, however, they will need to prepare performance descriptions for content statements found in the standards and in the extensive narrative that elaborates those standards.

These discontinuities in state assessment practices need to be recognized and considered as the process of planning standards-based lessons unfolds. Lead teachers, working in conjunction with the district's assessment coordinator, need to be vigilant and knowledgeable about state practices in standards assessment. These professionals can inform teachers of the best way to use state standards to prepare students for high-stakes testing.

Step 3: Describe Student Performances or Products

During the critical third step of the SAPC, teachers take each content statement selected from the frameworks in Step 2 and translate it into an active-voice description of a student performance or product. Each performance description becomes one of the lesson plan's objectives. The objectives are outcome behaviors that the teacher wants students to exhibit.

Using their frameworks and standards-aligned texts, which include suggested activities and detailed information about the selected content statements, teachers can readily compose descriptions of intended student outcomes. These observable behaviors or products are designed to meet the standards because they are written from content statements of the frameworks and standards. During this step, the teachers are in effect conducting a professional negotiation: The desired performances must be sufficiently rigorous to meet the learning expectations of the frameworks and at the same time be achievable by their students.

Mrs. Hernandez and her team write a performance description based on a content statement that they isolated from the framework in Step 2:

> Content statement: The life cycles of some insects consist of egg, larval, pupal, and adult stages.
>
> Performance description: Students *will label* pictures of the life cycle stages of a butterfly with correct stage names—egg, larval, pupal, and adult.

We see that the content statement includes only science facts. It does not describe what students will do to demonstrate knowledge of the facts. The second statement is a curriculum translation of the first. It describes student actions that will demonstrate knowledge of the facts. The inclusion of the verb *label* is a key element in this step, because the teacher can see the act of labeling pictures as students perform it. This act also results in a product that can be evaluated. The teachers have emphasized the importance of using an action verb by italicizing it.

The quality of the action required of the students is also important. In addition to the visibility of the performance or product, teachers will want to consider higher-level reasoning expectations for students as they explore the concepts. Stage labeling is a relatively low-level cognitive skill. Other visible actions or products written for this lesson should call for the application of higher-level reasoning skills.

Supplemental resources, including lists of behavioral verbs and example statements that include them, can guide teachers as they translate content statements from frameworks into high-quality performance descriptions. Most of these lists are responsive to the work of Benjamin Bloom (1956). Several interpretations of Bloom's taxonomy of educational objectives in the cognitive domain include sets of behavioral verbs that can be used to write higher-level reasoning tasks for students (see Figure 3.1). Many books and Web sites also provide valuable assistance in writing performance descriptions.[5]

As they develop higher-level expectations for their students, Mrs. Hernandez and her team decide to ask students to perform a more intellectually challenging task than simply labeling stage names properly. Their knowledge of curriculum resources enables the teachers to propose creative ideas that will produce desired performance outcomes. Prior experience with picture cards, for example,

FIGURE 3.1

Bloom's Taxonomy of Educational Objectives with Behavioral Verbs

Level of Cognition	Definition	Behavioral Verbs
Knowledge	Recognizes and remembers names, ideas, terms	*Name, label, describe, define, select*
Comprehension	Explains, summarizes, and makes simple interpretations	*Explain, predict, sort, distinguish between*
Application	Applies rules or procedures to novel situations	*Compute, solve, demonstrate*
Analysis	Identifies component parts; reasons deductively or inductively	*Discriminate, infer, diagram, resolve*
Synthesis	Puts disparate elements together to create a new idea or product	*Devise, generate, construct, compose*
Evaluation	Uses criteria to judge qualities of products or performances	*Contrast, discriminate, interpret, judge*

led the 2nd grade teachers to suggest that students sort the cards to demonstrate the order of the life cycle stages of frogs and butterflies. Mrs. Hernandez, aware of the book *The Very Hungry Caterpillar* (Carle, 2001) and its use as a prompt for story writing, proposed that students write brief stories of themselves growing up as butterflies or frogs. The teachers used knowledge of their curriculum resources to write the following performance description:

> Students *will write* a description of themselves growing up as a frog or a butterfly. They *will use* proper stage names and the academic language of the standard in their description.

The performance description includes a criterion of proficiency that students should meet as they write their paragraphs. The expectation of proper stage names and academic language in the outcome statement can be used as a criterion to evaluate students' work. When teachers specify in detail the nature of a desired response, clearly indicating the expected outcomes, they can use this description to determine whether any given student product has met the lesson's objectives.

Additionally, writing an original paragraph is a higher-level reasoning task than the labeling of stage names called for earlier. This expectation now also includes the science process standard, selected in Step 2 of the SAPC: "Students will write or draw descriptions of a sequence of steps, events, and observations." As mentioned at the end of that step, selected process statements from the standards and frameworks are most easily addressed when teachers are considering student behavior that will meet their expectations. When our three 2nd grade teachers review the process statement, it guides them to consider ways students can demonstrate their knowledge of life cycle stages. If students write about the stages or draw and label the stages in a manner that shows the correct sequence of stage development, they will be meeting the selected process statement as they demonstrate knowledge of the selected content statement.

As our teachers conclude this stage of the Planning Cycle, they move methodically through each of the content statements taken from the framework, translating them into descriptions of student performances or products. The teachers use a behavioral verb and at least one appropriate qualifying statement that together characterize an acceptable performance.

When concluded, this activity results in a set of student performance descriptions that will form the objectives of a standards-based lesson. The teachers then need to place the anticipated performances in a developmental sequence that matches the order in which students conduct them. As they select and sequence performance descriptions, they develop a shared vision of expected student performances that will meet the standards.

After preparing and selecting student performance descriptions for the intended lesson, Mrs. Hernandez and her colleagues will need to reexamine the framework's content statements to see that all expected student learning is expressed at an acceptable level of challenge. They also need to compare these content statements with the expectations of the performance descriptions they have written. Checking their final performance descriptions with the content statements that gave rise to them ensures that the teachers have not diverged from the intended learning of the standards and their elaborating statements. (This same concern will arise in the next step.)

In our work, Kimmel and I (O'Shea & Kimmel, 2003) have noted a tendency for performance descriptions to change emphasis as the lesson planning process moves forward. The performance descriptions sometimes move away from the intended learning described in the standards and toward the intentions included in commercial texts. This problem can be avoided if teachers check their developing plans against the learning expectations of the standards they originally intended to meet.

Step 4: Select and Sequence Learning Activities

After teachers refer to their curriculum resources to write performance descriptions in Step 3, they can use the same resources to select activities in Step 4. As Mrs. Hernandez and the other 2nd grade teachers begin this step of the Planning Cycle, they search for curriculum resources that will lead students to exhibit the behaviors described in the lesson's objectives. Teachers will continue to use their frameworks and texts during this step. High-quality curriculum resources can aid in the development of a logical, coherent sequence of activities that leads to expected student performances.

The lesson on life cycles can illustrate this point. Our three 2nd grade teachers came up with the idea for using activity cards to display the life cycle stages of frogs and butterflies because they were already familiar with similar cards included in their curriculum materials. Mrs. Hernandez found that a national publisher produces high-quality color pictures of frogs and butterflies in their various life cycle stages, complete with descriptive information about each stage printed on the back of the pictures. Her familiarity with the picture cards inspired some of the activities of the lesson.

Knowledgeable teachers will typically review resources on hand as they consider activities to elicit student performances, but difficulty arises if the school district's curriculum resources are inadequate. Teachers will need to move beyond their core curriculum resources when they encounter content statements in the frameworks that are not addressed by their materials. This often happens when the text covers some topics at one grade level, whereas the state's standards address the same topics at another grade level. During such times, teachers might consider the following options:

• gaining access to the publisher's curriculum materials for the grade level in which the content of the standard is conveyed

• using the Internet to explore the learning expectations of the framework that are not well covered by curriculum resources at hand

• turning to reference materials (textbooks for other age groups, encyclopedias, publishers' resources, media, and the like) to find appropriate resources for writing performance descriptions and preparing activities that will elicit desired student responses

Step 4 concludes once teachers have matched their selected activities with their list of student performance descriptions (see Figure 3.2). Will the planned activities lead students to demonstrate the behaviors and products described in the lesson objectives? This is the ultimate

FIGURE 3.2

Objectives and Activities of the Lesson Plan for 2nd Grade Science

Objectives:
- Given pictures of the life cycle stages of frogs and butter-flies, students *will place* them in proper order for each animal.
- Students *will list* the life cycle stages of frogs and butterflies in proper order.
- In a brief skit about the life of a frog or a butterfly, students *will describe* the features of the life cycle stage they are portraying.
- Following a reading of *The Very Hungry Caterpillar*, students *will write* a description of themselves growing up as a frog or a butterfly. They *will use* proper stage names and the academic language of the standards in their description.

Activities:
1. Show frog and butterfly activity cards; ask students to identify the animals; see whether students know any life cycle stages and their names.
2. Using the activity cards, reveal all stages of both animals in proper order; elicit student choral recitations of each stage name as it appears.
3. Show a video of the growth and development of the frog and the butterfly.
4. Have pairs of students sort shuffled activity cards into proper order for each animal.
5. Have pairs of students write a list of the life cycle stages in proper order for each animal, working from sorted picture cards.
6. Have several students line up in sequential order of the life cycle stages for each animal and ask them to describe the particular stage they are portraying. They will say what the animal eats and where it lives.

question that will be answered for our teachers only when they review student work products resulting from their lessons.

Step 5: Evaluate Student Performances and Products

To determine whether learning is progressing as planned, teachers evaluate their students' work, reviewing work samples to see whether they are complete. Experienced teachers examine student performances and products for two other purposes: (1) to inform students of their level of understanding of material just covered and (2) to evaluate the effectiveness of instruction to see whether adjustments need to be made.

In this last step of the SAPC, teachers use their lesson plan objectives to evaluate students' work. They do this individually, in the classroom as work is collected, and also collaboratively, in their grade-level or department planning sessions. How easy this task is depends on how the lesson plan objectives were written. Vague descriptions without qualifying statements and descriptions illustrating "good enough" performances leave teachers poorly equipped to make judgments about the quality of their students' work. In contrast, explicit performance descriptions with precise qualifying statements make the task of evaluating work a relatively straightforward one.

Mrs. Hernandez and her colleagues use the following performance description to evaluate students' work: "Students *will list* the life cycle stages of frogs and butterflies in proper order." The qualifying statement in this performance description is the phrase *in proper order.* With this statement in mind, the teachers examine each work sample to find a listing of butterfly and frog stages from egg to adult. This first performance description leaves little room for ambiguity.

Other performance descriptions in the life cycles lesson, however, are less useful for evaluating students' work. Consider a second performance description: "In a brief skit about the life of a frog or butterfly, students *will describe* the features of the life cycle stage they are portraying." This particular performance description does little to help a teacher evaluate students' work because it lacks qualifying statements about the features to be described.

Perhaps the performance description would be more useful as follows:

> In a brief skit about the life of a frog or butterfly, students *will portray* a life cycle stage and *identify* the stage by name, *stating* the stages that precede and follow it, and *stating* what the animal eats in this stage and where it lives.

Asking students to compare their life cycle stage with the one that follows or precedes it—in terms of anatomical features, relative motility, and sources of nutrition—leads to more precise evaluation. An objective with this level of detail is a useful tool for, specifically, evaluating a student's performance in a skit about butterflies or frogs.

Linking lesson objectives to student work evaluation makes the SAPC a process for continual instructional improvement. As teachers meet to discuss student performances and compare each performance to their predetermined expectations, they are checking student achievement of state standards. If students are meeting expectations, then student achievement on standards-based tests will follow in due course. When students do not meet expectations, reteaching or review may be necessary.

Challenges for Standards-Based Planning

The examples developed in this chapter were taken from California's standards documents. California has explicit content and process standards written for each grade level. Other states have different standards and supporting documents of varying quality, yet the fundamental processes of the SAPC apply in these settings as well. In New Jersey, for example, the directories of test specifications provide example performance descriptions that teachers can build upon to write their lesson objectives. California does not provide an equivalent document. The frameworks in New Jersey are less helpful than the frameworks in California because they include more teaching suggestions and fewer content descriptions.

Other state departments of education have posted student work samples that are useful for preparing performance descriptions. Teachers need time to learn the organization and content of their own state's standards documents before they can implement the SAPC to prepare standards-based lessons.

Can teachers use the SAPC to plan all of their lessons in one academic year? The answer is an unqualified no. A team of teachers may need 60 to 90 minutes to prepare a good standards-based lesson using the SAPC. Each teacher on a secondary school planning team may deliver 400 or more different lessons in one year. A planning team could prepare only 40 standards-based lessons in any one year. Clearly, then, teachers cannot plan all their lessons through the SAPC. Over the course of two or three years, though, a substantial number of lessons can be upgraded and made truly standards-based through a consistent application of the SAPC. The rate of lesson development can be substantially enhanced if teachers receive curriculum planning time during the summer.

The adage "A rising tide raises all ships" can apply to lesson planning and teaching when the SAPC becomes a weekly routine, not just a summertime occurrence. If teachers use the SAPC on a regular and consistent basis, their expectations for student learning will increase for all lessons they teach. The quality of all teaching and learning could be improved by such use of the SAPC.

Is Your School Ready for the Planning Cycle?

At Mariposa Elementary School, teachers learned the steps of the SAPC after the school district thoroughly prepared for the collaborative planning and teaching essential to the process. School leaders who would like to incorporate the SAPC into instruction should consider the preparations that need to take place before teachers are introduced to the collaborative lesson planning activities described in this chapter. Figure 3.3 provides a checklist to help guide the way for installing the SAPC in any elementary or secondary school where standards achievement is a desired goal.

FIGURE 3.3

Checklist for Adopting the Planning Cycle

Teachers have the following resources essential to standards-based planning:

_____ an understanding of the critical standards to be achieved in their teaching assignment

_____ a copy of the state standards including the critical standards selected by the district

_____ copies of the state frameworks in language arts, math, and other subjects for which state standards have been written

FIGURE 3.3   (continued)

_____ information about state standards assessments and the standards that are frequently assessed

_____ curriculum materials that are aligned with the current state standards

_____ guidelines for writing instructional objectives from standards and frameworks

The school is organized to accommodate the Standards Achievement Planning Cycle:

_____ Teachers have been organized into planning teams.

_____ Teams have been allocated 90 minutes of collaborative planning time per week.

_____ Supplemental curriculum planning resources, including Internet access, copies of Bloom's taxonomy, and guidelines for writing performance descriptions are available for planning teams.

_____ Each planning team is guided by the district's curriculum pacing guidelines and model lesson plans that display the features found in standards-meeting lessons.

Teachers have been trained to work collaboratively:

_____ Teachers can translate the learning expectations of their state standards into performance descriptions for student achievement of the standards.

_____ Teachers know how to include the academic language of the standards in the activities of their lessons.

_____ School leaders and curriculum specialists are available to planning teams and can assist them with their lesson planning activities.

4

The District's Plans for Standards Implementation

Chapter 1 provided an overview of the La Senda School District's planning activities and the numerous preparations that took place before teachers were trained in a new lesson planning protocol. In this chapter, we will see how the district's leadership team, under the superintendent's direction, built the capacity for standards-based teaching and learning.

Thorough preparation for effective standards-based teaching goes beyond the simple curriculum alignment and materials adoption strategies that are popular throughout the United States. It calls for a system of integrated resources and enabling conditions that supports teachers as they conduct standards-based planning and evaluation activities. We will begin our review of the district's preparations with a look at its communications plan. This plan set the stage for all subsequent reform activities.

Communicating the Need for Curriculum Reform

Dr. Castro, the superintendent of La Senda schools, recognized early in his career that successful advocacy for curriculum change depends on good communication with all parties. An effective communications plan anticipates the concerns and challenges that district constituents may raise when they learn about curriculum reform proposals. If the intentions of the reform effort are made known to the public and likely problems are acknowledged before they occur, reluctant and skeptical parties will be more likely to participate in planning activities. They may also exercise patience and reserve when problems arise during the reform installation process.

Dr. Castro knew that an effective communications plan would instill community confidence in the district's leadership. Principals and other administrators need to believe that teachers will follow their leadership when they advocate for changes in teaching practices. They also need to believe that it will make a difference for students if teachers focus their instructional planning on standards achievement. With these thoughts in mind, Dr. Castro shared his concerns about state standards with members of the La Senda Board of Education. He raised a number of key issues at board meetings and during informal conversations with school board members, influential teachers, and leaders of the community—long before changes in the school curriculum took place.

Promoting the Benefits of a Standards-Based School

Principals know they must demonstrate adequate yearly progress in standards achievement to meet the No Child Left Behind regulations, yet many teachers see content standards as an intrusion into their professional lives. School leaders need to overcome resistance to the standards movement by arguing persuasively for standards achievement. Promoting standards as part of a promising reform agenda, not an external mandate, Dr. Castro discussed the following benefits with his colleagues and community members:

• *State standards clarify local priorities for student learning.* Standards resolve questions concerning the scope and sequence of the curriculum. In some states, knowledge and skills of important subjects have been written for each grade level in elementary school and for content areas in secondary school. Arguments against teaching particular topics and skills become moot when the topics and skills are included in high-stakes tests administered by the state. High-stakes testing provides districts with the opportunity to move on with the important work of teaching content well, rather than resolving the problem of what to teach and when to teach it.

• *State standards help ensure that for the first time, high-stakes tests actually measure the curriculum that is taught.* Standardized testing, in contrast with standards-based testing, only compares the performance of the district's students with the performance of other students. Criterion-referenced standards-based exams measure each student's mastery of the essential knowledge of the district's curriculum when the curriculum is fully aligned with state standards. State content standards link classroom instruction, curriculum resources, and teaching efforts to the specific knowledge and skills covered on high-stakes tests.

• *The achievement gap between underperforming students and their more privileged counterparts is closing in many states where standards are well developed* (Haycock, 1998). Large numbers of poor and minority students are finally receiving the rich curriculum they deserve. Slowly, expectations for student learning are rising. Moreover, most of the states that have demonstrated improvement on the National Assessment of Educational Progress are also states with well-developed standards and assessments (Skinner & Staresina, 2004).

• *National and state accountability movements are based on student achievement of state standards.* The No Child Left Behind Act requires districts to demonstrate adequate yearly progress in the achievement of state standards as assessed by state tests. School districts that successfully convey their state's standards will see their students perform well on the high-stakes exams.

• *National textbook publishers have begun to align their products with state standards.* As time passes, published curriculum materials will align more accurately with the scope and sequence of the district's curriculum because the curriculum is aligned with the state standards that are driving textbook change.

Dr. Castro experienced little difficulty in persuading the La Senda board members to support needed changes in the curriculum. Asking the board of education to support standards-based lesson planning and student work evaluation, which would require more planning time and professional development for teachers, was another matter. Dr. Castro approached this task by turning to the research that supports the essential components of the SAPC.

Presenting Research That Supports the Planning Cycle

Dr. Castro knew that school board members and community members needed assurance that student achievement of the standards would result if funds were expended on professional development and increased planning time for teachers. He approached this challenge by finding evidence that the strategies soon to be proposed would be effective in raising student achievement. He described the national and international research that supports the process of collaborative lesson planning and work evaluation that makes up the SAPC. This research base includes the studies that we examined in Chapter 2:

• A statewide research project in Oregon conducted by Tell, Bodone, and Addie (2000) demonstrated the value of planning lessons from standards documents instead of simply teaching from curriculum materials.

• The work of Resnick and Nolan (1995) delineated the planning tools teachers need for truly functional standards.

• The Third International Mathematics and Science Study revealed the merits of teacher collaboration during lesson planning and student work evaluation (Willis, 2002) and highlighted the value of these activities as they appear in Japanese Lesson Study (Lewis & Tsuchida, 1998).

• The findings of Black and William (1998), Nave, Miech, and Mosteller (2000), and Ogawa, Sandholtz, Martinez-Flores, and Scribner (2003) showed the need for a specific instructional technology that connects the standards to improved student learning.

Dr. Castro was able to demonstrate that the SAPC is a logical bridge connecting state standards resources and curriculum materials to expected learning outcomes required by No Child Left Behind. The SAPC is supported by both theory and practice and is grounded in research. Dr. Castro worked to convey this important message to key district stakeholders prior to announcing the formation of a districtwide curriculum committee for standards achievement.

Discussing the Standards Implementation Process

Dr. Castro's journey toward effective standards implementation began with cabinet meetings in which principals and curriculum leaders agreed to a coherent plan to address state and national accountability challenges based on content standards. Following the meetings, Dr. Castro included the La Senda Board of Education in a professional development program for district leaders. The program stressed the importance of the state content standards and their place in the current educational reform environment. This conversation was followed by a public session of the board dedicated to state content standards and the district's curriculum. Finally, the president of the board of education and Dr. Castro publicly appointed a highly visible committee to develop a districtwide plan for standards implementation. Reflecting the K–12 structure of the school district, the committee was composed of

- the assistant superintendent for curriculum and instruction
- a board of education member
- the principal of the middle school
- a high school teacher and leader in the local teachers' union
- Mrs. Lewis, in her capacity as an elementary school principal
- Mrs. Hernandez, a 2nd grade teacher
- a parent and leader of a community-based organization
- a high school student

Committee members encouraged the participation of all district constituents. Through this open process, political capital for the reform effort arose from community understanding of the need for change.

Holding Community Meetings to Build Support

The committee invited community members to the planning process through two kinds of public sessions. The first type included formal evening presentations and noontime brown bag lunches at elementary schools that serve all the district's attendance zones. This approach is similar to the strategy used by many well-managed districts as they approach the dreaded task of redistricting. At these meetings, the committee described the need for districtwide reform to initiate standards-based teaching and learning. Parents and community members voiced their concerns, and the committee accepted their suggestions.

The second kind of session included informal neighborhood gatherings at community organizations and church facilities. Influential community leaders hosted discussions about proposed changes in the curriculum and school attendance schedules. This approach worked well for communities that had been traditionally alienated from the public school system. Dr. Castro understood that these community meetings would help build support for the change process that was coming.

Following the meetings, community suggestions and concerns were acknowledged and included, where appropriate, in the final reform plan. The reform agenda, which is shown in Figure 4.1 (on p. 68), balanced responsibility for needed changes among the board of education, district administration, and teachers as a whole.

Approving the Reform Agenda

The committee members submitted the agenda to the district administration and the La Senda Board of Education, which adopted it in formal session. After the board accepted the reform agenda, responsibility for enacting it was transferred to district leaders. The reform agenda embraced the enabling conditions described in Chapter 2. Dr. Castro was successful in showing the board members that the enabling conditions would need to be installed in the La Senda School District if teachers were to be successful with the SAPC.

A new executive committee of district personnel was appointed to put the agenda into action. Members of the new committee were

FIGURE 4.1

Model Agenda for Standards-Based Reform

1. Change school schedules to provide teachers with the time needed for collaborative planning and student work evaluation.

2. Select essential state standards for each grade level and subject.

3. Align curriculum guides with the scope and sequence of the selected standards.

4. Add standards pacing information to each of the curriculum guides.

5. Use standards, frameworks, and the new curriculum guides to select texts and other curriculum materials.

6. Develop a coherent system of assessments that measures standards achievement without imposing more test time on teachers and students.

assigned to co-lead subcommittees—composed of administrators, teachers, and resource personnel—that would be responsible for developing each agenda item. The committee monitored the progress of the subcommittees and coordinated their combined efforts. The six goals of the reform agenda were realized through introducing a new class scheduling model, selecting a set of state standards targeted for student achievement, creating truly functional curriculum guides, and implementing an effective process for adopting curriculum materials aligned with the district's standards-based curriculum.

Scheduling Collaborative Planning Time

The subcommittee charged with scheduling planning time for teacher collaboration had to overcome the established tradition of teacher isolation. In the United States, the lack of sufficient collaborative planning time has been a major obstacle to structural reform. In contrast, 99 percent of all elementary school teachers and 50 percent of middle school teachers in Japan participate in lesson study groups that meet two to five hours per week (National Commission on Mathematics and Science Teaching for the 21st Century, 2000). During their planning time, Japanese teachers collaborate in designing lessons and reviewing students' work.

Teachers in the La Senda schools would need time to work together to conduct the SAPC. Dr. Castro knew that teachers would be more likely to accept their new roles and responsibilities in standards-based teaching after they realized that the school district was making a commitment to additional planning time at the beginning of the change process. The subcommittee charged with revising school schedules included teachers' union representatives, which created goodwill and increased the political capital of the administration as it moved forward with the remainder of the reform agenda. The subcommittee eventually recommended that grade-level teams in elementary schools meet once a week for approximately one and a half hours to conduct SAPC activities. Students at these schools would be released for one afternoon during the school week. The middle school and high school schedules would also need adjustment, and the subcommittee considered three different options.

The first option required a school building with learning areas of various sizes, including media rooms and recreation areas. In this kind of building, large- and small-group scheduling can be organized so teachers have time to work together. Two or three teachers can supervise a large group of students in an assembly or study hall while other teachers meet in planning teams. Later in the week, these roles may be reversed, allowing all teachers at least 90 minutes a week to work through the SAPC. Abington Junior High School in Abington, Pennsylvania, was designed for this kind of scheduling. Large-, medium-, and small-group meeting rooms are available throughout the building for creative scheduling arrangements. In Dr. Castro's district, however, this option was not feasible because of the conventional nature of the high school building. The scheduling subcommittee turned its attention to a second option.

In this second approach, class sessions can be reduced by a small amount of time at the beginning and end of the day to accommodate longer periods in the middle of the day. Students can attend lunch, laboratory-based instruction, or performing arts classes during these extended periods while teachers of subjects with content standards can plan together at the same time. After receiving input from high school teachers and student representatives, the subcommittee dismissed this option and settled on the third approach: block scheduling.

The committee chose a method of block scheduling that met the district's needs. In this model, students attend different classes on alternate days (so-called A and B days). Teachers with the same subject assignment can have the same extended period of time to plan together on either an A day or a B day. If teachers have five classes to teach and the school day includes three classes, then one extended planning period is available to every teacher on either an A or a B day. Principal Candy McCarthy of Alisal High School in Salinas, California, has used her school's block scheduling to bring teachers together for collaborative planning. For example, the mathematics teachers are able to meet twice weekly to plan lessons or review students' work.

Dr. Castro and his colleagues took every opportunity to explain the intended purpose of the additional planning time to school staff and community members, thereby building trust in the reform movement. When the scheduling subcommittee presented Dr. Castro with the block scheduling option, he knew that a skeptical public would want information on what teachers would be doing with their additional planning time. He addressed these concerns by describing the activities of lesson planning and student work evaluation and giving frequent updates about the reform agenda during public board meetings. He also made a point of describing the need for standards-based teaching and learning to the education reporter of the local newspaper. A special newsletter about planned changes was sent home with students. Through such frequent communications, parents soon realized that the quality of instructional time is at least as important to student learning as the quantity of time spent in classrooms.

Selecting Essential State Standards

In almost every state, the knowledge and skills conveyed at various grade levels, or in particular subjects, have been determined by state authorities with the power to enforce change of practice through high-stakes testing. Now that these changes have taken place across the United States, the selection of essential content standards for each grade level and for each course needs to proceed at the district level.

Dr. Castro's subcommittee for standards selection and alignment had a number of issues to address before standards could be identified for each grade level and core subject across the district.

Too Many Standards?

The first task of the subcommittee for standards selection and alignment was to deal with the problem of excessive standards. Robert Marzano, an acknowledged expert in standards-based education, has prescribed a clearly needed change to improve state standards and student achievement: "Cut the number of standards and

---

Standards? What Standards?

So many standards have been produced for so many purposes that it is hard to identify which are most important to guide student learning. First came the national curriculum standards in important subjects, including math, science, and social studies. The first national curriculum standards, the curriculum standards of the National Council of Teachers of Mathematics, led to reforms in mathematics education. Many publishers and some states prepared math curricula guided by these standards.

Professional teaching standards have also been written. In many states, teachers are encouraged to obtain certification through the National Board for Professional Teaching Standards. Colorado and California have produced their own professional teaching standards. The *California Standards for the Teaching Profession,* for example, identifies the skills and knowledge to be acquired by teacher candidates in approved teacher preparation programs.[1]

State academic content standards for public school students in preschool through grade 12 are the relevant standards in the current reform environment, because they are the source material for the content included in high-stakes examinations now required in most states. In this book, the focus is on these state standards. They declare what students are to know and be able to do with important subject matter. They are also the standards used to measure adequate yearly progress required by No Child Left Behind regulations. In many settings, the tests that measure the achievement of these standards are used to determine whether students are to be retained in a grade, whether high school students will graduate, or how much funding a school will receive. School districts need to know the important distinctions between national standards and state content standards in the current accountability environment.

the content within standards dramatically." He describes how excessive state standards have set unrealistic expectations for teachers. "To cover all this content, you would have to change schooling from K–12 to K–22. By my reckoning, we would have to cut content by about two-thirds" (Scherer, 2001, pp. 14, 15).

With the exception of a few states that have thoughtfully reduced their standards to an achievable body of knowledge, the overabundance of standards means that some standards will not be taught. In the La Senda School District, the standards selection subcommittee involved several teachers in the process of choosing important standards. Although teacher involvement was essential, the administration had to take responsibility for ensuring that teachers of the same grade level or subject were using the same sets of standards. That is, the process of selecting important standards must be both collaborative and centralized.

The subcommittee recognized that curriculum management could not develop across the district if teachers could not agree to teach the same set of standards. If the teachers of U.S. history in the district high school could not agree to teach certain standards, then one teacher could end up teaching California History–Social Science Standard 11.2 on industrialization and immigration, while another teacher, ignoring that standard, could spend the same time in the semester addressing Standard 11.4 on the role of the United States as a world power.

Under these circumstances, students taking the same course from different instructors would learn from different standards, and their relative abilities to perform well on state standards exams would depend on their class section enrollment rather than their efforts to achieve a uniform set of standards. In the La Senda schools, selecting proper sets of standards for all grade levels and subjects was a major task requiring a year of coordinated faculty deliberations.

Which Standards Are Important?

The La Senda teachers and administrators had strong feelings about the essential knowledge and skills that students should acquire. Dr. Castro recommended that the subcommittee members read Wiggins and McTighe's (1998) book, *Understanding by Design,* to help guide the standards selection process. The authors discuss *enduring understandings,* the important ideas that can have lasting value for learners. Although the La Senda subcommittee looked for standards that included enduring understandings, they also needed to pragmatically consider the standards most likely to be assessed on state exams. The subcommittee thus sought to identify standards of enduring value as well as standards of significance in the state accountability system. The subcommittee, with the assistance of teachers from a variety of subjects and grade levels, used two types of resources as they moved forward: (1) national and state resources to find enduring standards and (2) state resources to identify tested standards.

How to Identify Enduring Standards

National curriculum standards provide rich descriptions of the central concepts of disciplines taught in public schools. The standards derive from the wisdom of scholars in social studies, literature, science, and mathematics. National standards are useful for guiding the selection of related state standards to form a coherent scope and sequence in a given discipline. State standards that include the knowledge and skills of national curriculum standards are likely to have enduring value for learners.

Consider this statement from the curriculum standards of the National Council for the Social Studies (1994):

> The study of people, places, and human-environment interactions assists learners as they create their spatial views and geographic perspectives of the world. Today's social, cultural, economic, and civic demands on individuals mean that students will need the knowledge, skills, and understanding to ask and answer questions such as: Where are things located? Why are they located where they are? What patterns are reflected in the groupings of things? What do we mean by region?[2]

The national social studies curriculum standards include several strands that form major themes of history and geography. We may reasonably infer that the above is a concept of enduring value because it is one of a few major conceptual themes of the social studies identified by nationally recognized scholars.

Now consider this related core curriculum content standard and indicator from the New Jersey Department of Education (2004):

6.6 All students will apply knowledge of spatial relationships and other geographic skills to understand human behavior in relation to the physical and cultural environment.

   A.1 Explain the spatial concepts of location, distance, and direction, including:
         The location of school, home, neighborhood, community, state, and country
         The relative location of the community and the places within it
         The location of continents and oceans[3]

Comparing the New Jersey standard with the national standard, we see that they are similar in content but different in richness of ideas for teaching. On one hand, the national standard is a useful resource for the interpretation of the related state standard. On the other hand, the state standard is confirmed in its importance by its relationship to the national curriculum for the social studies. Clearly, New Jersey's social studies standard and its related cumulative progress indicator include understandings of enduring value.

How to Identify Tested Standards

States vary in the extent to which they disclose information about specific standards that will appear on their exams. Some states provide Web sites with valuable information about their state tests, including test blueprints. The following questions focused the subcommittee's search for critical standards to be included in each grade level and subject:

• Are some categories of standards tested more consistently than others?

• Can we identify specific standards within these categories that are more likely to appear on state tests?

• Are there critical standards that have been assessed by two or more questions on recently administered exams?

• Which standards go untested year after year?

• Can we predict the standards that will be assessed on this year's test?

The standards selection subcommittee for the La Senda schools became familiar with the essential state resources to use in the standards selection process. They learned, for instance, that test blueprints are available from the Web site of the California Department of Education. Other states also provide useful information for this process. By example, we will look at the information available to educators in Virginia.

On its Web site, the Commonwealth of Virginia Department of Education provides valuable tools to help school districts find frequently tested standards, including sample scope and sequence tables. Copies of past examinations and sample test items are also available on the Web site.[4]

Test blueprints are another useful resource. For instance, the *Blueprint, Grade 5, Mathematics Test* (Commonwealth of Virginia, 2003) provides insights into Standards of Learning that are likely to be assessed on state exams. The blueprint introduction explains how educators in Virginia can use the blueprints to select critical standards. It includes specific information about Standards of Learning that are covered on state tests and about the number of test items that appear in each reporting category and on the test as a whole. For example, the blueprint reveals that the computation and estimation category of the math test will include 25 percent more items than the number and number sense category. This information can be used to determine the amount of time and emphasis that teachers will apply to planning and teaching standards in each of these categories.

Copies of tests posted on the Virginia Department of Education site can be analyzed to identify specific standards that have been tested in the past. This analysis will reveal patterns of changing emphasis on state tests, but it cannot identify the specific standards to be assessed on the next test. Educators in Virginia can predict the likelihood that any one of the Standards of Learning will be tested based on patterns of testing seen in the past in conjunction with information provided by the blueprints.

Other states offer different kinds of information about their standards exams. New Jersey, for example, provides directories of test specifications that include more information than Virginia's blueprints. A test matrix displays the percentage of test items attributed to certain categories of standards, but the level of detail makes it possible to infer the percentage of items for each standard. We can also see the distribution of items by cognitive challenge level (e.g., knowledge and comprehension, critical thinking and problem solving). Sample test questions are also provided by the New Jersey Department of Education. These New Jersey documents are particularly useful because they include skill and knowledge statements that describe student performances that meet the standards.

The standards selection subcommittee in the La Senda School District used information posted on the California Department of Education Web site to identify the standards that were likely to be tested. The district then began aligning the curriculum with the selected standards. This task called for major changes in the school district's approved curriculum guides.

Aligning Curriculum Guides with the Standards

School district curriculum policy usually takes the form of curriculum guides that describe the skills and knowledge taught in various grades and subjects. One of the subcommittees for the La Senda schools was assigned to align the district's curriculum guides with the critical standards selected by the district. As the alignment process got under way, district staff had to move some topics and skills to other grade levels or subjects where related standards were to be taught and tested. This task, when completed, resulted in an outline of skills and topics for each grade level and subject derived from corresponding standards.

The subcommittee knew that some teachers or curriculum leaders might object to changes in the curriculum guides when they recognized that their most treasured resources and activities were not going to be used in their teaching assignment. The entire success of the reform effort rested on the alignment of curriculum with the scope and sequence of the selected standards. The district had to reallocate curriculum resources and teaching staff to ensure coverage of essential content as dictated by the state testing schedule. The needs of the students had to prevail in this regard.

Avoiding Nominal Alignment

Curriculum alignment is one of the most common ways that districts are responding to the standards reform mandate. Unfortunately, too many districts have conducted only nominal alignment by simply inserting an additional line of related standards into an existing scope and sequence table. Figure 4.2 (on p. 78) provides an example of such nominal alignment. The curriculum guide excerpt is similar to materials recommended for use by the Virginia Department of Education. The SOL (Standards of Learning) entry identifies the state standards matched to content for the particular content/skills. The standards have been arranged to match related topics, rather than vice versa. The scope and sequence of the curriculum is not altered to reflect the coherent development of the standards.

Curriculum guides do little good if teachers do not value them as high-quality reference tools for teaching. The SOL entry is of little or no value because it does not convey meaningful information to the teacher. Similarly, the classroom assessment entry does not suggest specific strategies appropriate to the given standard. The general items listed in the resources are not applicable to the specific learning tasks of the teaching unit. In these regards, the example adapted from Virginia's scope and sequence table illustrates only nominal alignment.

Focusing on the Standards

In contrast to Figure 4.2, Figure 4.3 (on p. 79) presents an example of curriculum alignment with the standards. This sample was developed from the New Jersey core curriculum content standards for science and from related state documents. The guide includes the complete narrative of a standard, not just a code. The knowledge and skill statements have been transcribed from the standard's performance indicator found in the science directory of test specifications. The performance expectations include some expected student products or behaviors that demonstrate achievement of the standard. The resources entry identifies specific pages and materials in the district's curriculum resources that will help the teacher and students achieve the identified standard.

FIGURE 4.2

Nominal Alignment in a Curriculum Guide

Teaching Unit	Linear equations and inequalities
Content/Skills	Solve multistep equations by using • commutative properties • associative properties (other principles follow)
Related SOL	A.1, A.3
Classroom Assessment Methods	• Individual quizzes • Tests • Projects • Investigations • Portfolios • Student presentations • Questioning strategies • Peer evaluations
Resources	• Mathematics SOL • Teacher Resource Guide (Web site given) • SOL test blueprints • SOL test-released items • Virginia Algebra Resource Center (Web site given) • NASA and other agencies (Web sites given)

Figure 4.3 provides meaningful information and suggestions for standards-based teaching. The La Senda curriculum alignment subcommittee devised a new curriculum guide of this nature. It was structured to specifically function as a resource tool for teachers as they work together to plan standards-based lessons.

Adding Standards Pacing Information to the Guides

Curriculum guides are most useful when they include pacing information in addition to state standards. Teachers in New Jersey could use the curriculum guide excerpt in Figure 4.3 to pace their SAPC activities with the simple addition of one more entry that includes

FIGURE 4.3

Curriculum Guide Focused on Standards Achievement

Selected Standard	5.5 All students will gain an understanding of the structure, characteristics, and basic needs of organisms.
Selected Cumulative Progress Indicator	10. Identify and describe the structure and function of cell parts.
Knowledge/Skill Statements from Directory	• Cells carry on many functions needed to sustain life. • Cells are the units of structure and function of living things.
Sample Performance Expectations	• Label cell parts • Describe cell part functions • Distinguish between animal and plant cell parts
Resources	• Text reading: Unit 4, pp. 120–128 • Animal and plant cell diagrams • "Life of Cell" video

standards achievement dates (see Figure 4.4 on p. 80). This new information can assist teachers and administrators with curriculum management because it includes deadlines scheduled during the academic year when selected standards should be conveyed. With this information, teachers know when they should complete the teaching of a standard and have student work samples available for group analysis. Teachers will also know when the district will assess student mastery of each of the standards through the administration of a districtwide benchmark test.

Figure 4.4 informs teachers that they are to have student work samples ready for collaborative review on October 20. On November 16, a benchmark test covering this standard and other related standards will be administered in all biology classes in the district where Standard 5.6 is expected to be achieved. Benchmark tests inform teachers, students, parents, and administrators of the progress that

FIGURE 4.4

Curriculum Guide with Standards Achievement Dates

Selected Standard	5.5 All students will gain an understanding of the structure, characteristics, and basic needs of organisms.
Selected Cumulative Progress Indicator	10. Identify and describe the structure and function of cell parts.
Knowledge/Skill Statements from Directory	• Cells carry on many functions needed to sustain life. • Cells are the units of structure and function of living things.
Sample Performance Expectations	• Label cell parts • Describe cell part functions • Distinguish between animal and plant cell parts
Resources	• Text reading: Unit 4, pp. 120–128 • Animal and plant cell diagrams • "Life of Cell" video
Pacing Guide Achievement Dates	• October, week #2 • Student work products expected for completion by October 20 • Benchmark test: November 16

students are making in standards achievement throughout the academic year. Year-end testing has important uses, but it cannot reveal shortcomings in standards achievement in time for teachers to address their students' needs.

Determining Ideal Time Intervals

The time intervals for standards achievement need to be long enough to allow for variations in student rates of learning but brief enough to ensure that all standards selected for the academic year are conveyed. Teachers of the relevant subjects should meet to identify the number of standards to be assessed during a benchmark test and the amount of time to be allocated to the teaching of each standard. Experience with this process in California suggests that time allotment is a contentious issue: Some teachers will believe that they are not receiving enough time to convey certain standards. Deadlines should be set in the curriculum guide with the understanding that they may need to be revised based on teacher feedback.

In the La Senda School District, the subcommittee for curriculum alignment sought teachers' input regarding the amount of time needed for the achievement of selected standards. As a result of this collaborative planning, the subcommittee was able to estimate when critical standards would be achieved throughout the academic year. Effective curriculum management for standards achievement depends on this level of specificity and uniformity.

Supplementing the Curriculum Guide

A well-prepared curriculum guide will help teachers select critical standards, find resources for teaching the standards, and decide when standards should be taught and when students' work should be collected for group analysis. Figure 4.4 presents a portion of a hypothetical standards-based curriculum guide for teachers in New Jersey. Unfortunately, it provides only partial information for planning lessons and analyzing students' work. Therefore, in addition to the guide, teachers in New Jersey will need the core curriculum content standards, framework, and directory of test specifications for a given content area to fully prepare lessons with good performance expectations for their students. They should also use the national science education standards to ensure richness of learning.

Teachers will be able to supplement the guide with a growing compendium of lesson plans after they begin to conduct the SAPC on a regular basis. They can also collect samples of exemplary student work, accompanied by teacher commentary that identifies the high-quality elements of the samples. Teachers can use these examples to describe the essential features of a proficient performance to subsequent groups of students so that students can more readily excel. Samples of exemplary student work with teacher commentary also help teachers move through the SAPC quickly because they can evaluate students' work more efficiently.

Collaboratively developed lesson plans, exemplary samples of students' work with teacher commentary, and rubrics for assessing major student products will enrich the utility of the guide and thus increase the likelihood that teachers will conduct the SAPC regularly. These enhancements to the curriculum guide ensure the district administration that its key curriculum policy documents are being used to plan instruction—for the first time in many districts. Figure 4.5 identifies several of the features that can be found in a well-resourced curriculum guide after teachers have added products from their SAPC deliberations. As teachers work together to build their guides into teaching resources, they will grow as a team and increase their ability to help their students achieve the standards.

Choosing Curriculum Materials

School districts have traditionally used many important criteria to select curriculum resources for teachers and students, such as readability and the quality of content organization, student exercises, and instructional activities. Alignment with state content standards is the new criterion of interest to school leaders.

The publishing industry is struggling to keep up with the standards movement. Textbooks are written for a national market, but standards vary from state to state. Publishers have responded to variation in state standards by augmenting their core materials with supplementary resources in states where textbook sales volume is substantial. Schools in heavily populated states such as Texas and California benefit from this practice, whereas schools in the lesser populated Montana and Mississippi do not. States without large student populations and centralized curriculum adoption policies are left to choose from supplementary materials developed for the Texas and California markets.

Marketplace constraints make textbook adoption for standards achievement a difficult task to perform well. A textbook in 4th grade

FIGURE 4.5

Components of Effective Curriculum Guides and Planning Resources

Curriculum scope and sequence tables should include

- critical standards to be achieved in each subject and grade level
- essential content and skill statements extracted from frameworks, blueprints, and other state resources
- references to aligned curriculum resources with specific page numbers
- pacing columns in the curriculum guides that determine when all standards are to be achieved and when students' work should be submitted for group analysis
- deadline dates for the achievement of sets of standards to be evaluated through benchmark testing
- sample student performance descriptions that constitute proficiency

Additional resources are needed beyond the elements of the tables, including

- rubrics that describe substandard, standards-meeting, and proficient performances for major projects and units
- exemplary activities and teaching suggestions that will elicit standards-meeting performances from students
- lesson and unit plans developed by teachers that have resulted in high-quality student work
- examples of proficient and exemplary student work
- teacher commentary about the work samples that identifies their quality elements
- sample benchmark test questions from the district pool of items used in benchmark testing
- adopted curriculum materials to be used by teachers and students in meeting each standard

social studies is unlikely to be well aligned to all the 4th grade academic content standards in every state. Fortunately, a standards-based curriculum guide can help school districts select resources aligned with their state's standards.

The scope and sequence tables of standards-based curriculum guides are powerful tools for guiding textbook selection. In the La Senda School District, a separate subcommittee was charged with the responsibility of creating materials adoption guidelines using the new curriculum guides. Three attributes of the district's curriculum guides helped in this regard:

• clearly identified critical standards to be achieved in each grade level and in secondary school subjects

• student performance descriptions that explain what students will do to demonstrate achievement of each critical standard

• standards achievement pacing information that identifies the order and rate for achievement of the standards

Addressing District Standards in Appropriate Grades

Even in California, nationally produced grade school curriculum materials will not align with all of a district's selected standards in each of the elementary grades. The content and skills of the district's 5th grade social studies standards may very well appear in resources intended for the 3rd, 4th, or 6th grades. A publisher's 4th grade language arts resource may cover only 60 percent of the district's 4th grade standards. It may also encompass standards of other grades where the resource is not intended for use.

The La Senda School District's text adoption committee had to settle on the best match between the district's elementary grade-level standards and the scope and sequence of related content found in an elementary series. In some instances, teachers in different grades exchanged their materials to ensure coverage of all selected grade-level standards in accordance with the pacing information.

The subcommittee found that the district's secondary school textbooks are more closely aligned with selected standards, as would be expected. Most state standards for high school subjects are conveyed in a single course. By contrast, nationally produced elementary school textbooks may address content standards of different states at various grade levels. A good high school chemistry textbook is likely to include material that covers each of the district-selected chemistry standards.

Meeting Student Performance Expectations

Sample performance descriptions are an important element of the scope and sequence tables in standard-aligned curriculum guides. These statements describe what teachers will expect their students to minimally produce or perform as they demonstrate achievement of a standard. The performance expectations in Figure 4.4 indicate that students need to know how to label cell parts, describe cell part functions, and distinguish between animal and plant cell parts. As teachers examine curriculum resources, they will be looking for information that will enable students to perform these tasks at the stated grade level of the standard. When teachers review a variety of materials and evaluate them against the performance descriptions for selected standards, they will be able to isolate the resources most closely aligned with the critical standards of their district.

If we are satisfied that the topics and skills of a prospective resource are well aligned with the scope and sequence of the district's selected standards, we can move to the important task of evaluating the quality of the content and exercises that convey several of the standards. The subcommittee's next task was to assess the extent to which the content and exercises of a prospective resource would lead students to produce the sample performances described in the scope and sequence tables of the curriculum guide.

Consider the following example. If the La Senda textbook adoption committee had been working from the curriculum guide in Figure 4.4, they would have reviewed the three student performance expectations for meeting the standards: (1) label cell parts, (2) describe cell part functions, and (3) distinguish between animal and plant cell parts. The committee would have examined the content and exercises of various textbooks to see whether students would be provided with the information and skills needed to perform these tasks. Clearly, information and diagrams of animal and plant cells, including cell parts and their functions, have to appear in resources under consideration if students are to meet the performance expectations of the selected standard. The textbook adoption committee members would need to inspect the content related to several performance descriptions in their effort to find the text resources most likely to help students produce standards-meeting work. This critical step in the adoption process goes well beyond assessment of topic coverage.

Quality curriculum resources will do more than cover the content statements of many standards: They will guide students to the production of standards-meeting work as described in a district's curriculum guides. However, in a summer 2003 review of California social studies and science textbooks, I found that many state-approved texts included poor-quality exercises and end-of-chapter assessments. The exercises often failed to reach the cognitive challenge expected by the standards. This finding was particularly troubling because the reviewed texts had been judged by state educators to be well aligned with the standards. In many instances, standards content was reasonably well presented in the body of the texts, but the work expected of students was below the proficiency levels identified in the frameworks. In some state-approved texts, students were expected to perform word searches and sentence completion exercises. Such simple activities should not be included in the sample performance descriptions of a district's curriculum guides.

Textbook adoption committees should compare the student performance descriptions in their curriculum guides with the work expected of students in the textbooks under consideration. Only curriculum resources that have student achievement expectations in keeping with those of the standards should be considered for adoption.

Matching the Scope and Sequence of Pacing Information

When textbooks and other resources are being considered for adoption, pacing information within a district's curriculum guide can be useful in identifying the best offerings. Good pacing information will describe for teachers the order in which each standard should be achieved and the relative amount of time to be dedicated to teaching the content of the standard. Textbooks and other resources that are best matched to the district's standards-based curriculum will present subject matter at the same grade level of the pacing information, in the same developmental sequence of the selected standards, and with the same degree of emphasis on topics as suggested by the time line of the pacing guide. Such resources are easier for teachers to use and more likely to assist them and their students in achieving the district's selected state standards.

Is Your District Ready for the Planning Cycle?

This chapter describes the work that was done by the La Senda School District as its various committees prepared to install standards-based teaching and learning through a comprehensive program. These enabling preparations had to take place before teachers and administrators learned their respective roles and responsibilities to sustain standards-based teaching and learning in all the district's classrooms.

The preparatory activities described in this chapter will need to be accomplished in real-life districts as well before professional development can take place. The checklist in Figure 4.6 will help administrators assess the extent to which their district has the current capacity to install the SAPC and support teachers in its performance.

FIGURE 4.6

Checklist for Standards Implementation at the District Level

_____ The board of education has adopted a plan for changing curriculum and teaching practices for standards achievement.

_____ Parents, community members, and students are included in the planning process.

_____ Political support for the needed changes has been obtained from principals, lead teachers, the teachers' union, parents, and community members.

_____ Committees and subcommittees have been created to enact the district's agenda that prepares schools for standards implementation.

_____ Every school in the district has allocated a minimum of 90 minutes of weekly, uninterrupted planning time for teachers to meet in grade-level or subject-matter teams to conduct the Standards Achievement Planning Cycle.

_____ A districtwide standards selection subcommittee and its task forces have identified the critical state standards to be conveyed at each grade level and in each subject.

(continued)

FIGURE 4.6   (continued)

_____ The district's curriculum guides have been organized around the scope and sequence of selected standards, content statements from frameworks, and student performance descriptions; matching instructional resources have been included for each standard in the guide.

_____ Pacing information has been incorporated into the curriculum guides, including date ranges and deadlines for teachers to achieve each standard.

_____ The pacing information lets teachers know when to review student work samples and when benchmark tests will be administered.

_____ The district adopts only curriculum resources that are aligned with the district's selected critical standards and curriculum guides.

5

The Principal's Role in a Standards-Based School

In Chapter 4, we examined the role of the district in the standards implementation process. In this chapter, we will look closely at the efforts of Mrs. Lewis, the principal of Mariposa Elementary School, to prepare for, install, and sustain the Standards Achievement Planning Cycle. Some of her experiences included proposing changes in the school schedule, acquiring planning resources, advocating for upcoming changes in curriculum practices, and supporting teachers' early efforts with the SAPC. After teachers adjusted to the new routines, Mrs. Lewis introduced a modified instructional supervision process intended to sustain teachers' efforts with the SAPC.

Preparing the School Community for Change

Following her training, Mrs. Lewis realized that a lot of work needed to be done if teachers were to get off to a good start applying the skills of the SAPC. Each teacher would need time and resources for planning, plus colleagues to help along the way. Mrs. Lewis worked in concert with other principals to advocate for necessary changes among teachers, community members, and students. She also learned how to assist collaborative teams as a result of her own professional development with lead teachers of her school.

Mrs. Lewis knew that the first month following SAPC training for teachers would be crucial to a successful installation of new roles and responsibilities. The momentum and enthusiasm arising from professional development in new planning, teaching, and work evaluation skills would soon wane if these skills were not applied quickly to regular classroom practice. Teachers would need immediate access to essential resources as they moved from a training mode to the implementation of the SAPC in grade-level teams. Time was the most important resource.

The principal worked with central administrators to organize the school schedule around needed planning time. They accepted a committee's recommendation to release students from classes on Wednesday afternoons in all the district's elementary schools. As a result of this change, teachers would be free to conduct SAPC activities each Wednesday from 1:00 to 2:30 p.m. The district began an after-school recreation and academic program on Wednesday afternoons to help children of working parents.

Next, the administrators addressed teachers' planning needs. A complete set of planning resources was made available to each grade-level team so that teachers could work with the resources privately or in team sessions. At Mariposa Elementary School, the library/media center became a repository for all essential standards-based planning materials, including

- revised curriculum guides for subjects taught with content standards
- state content standards for each subject in the guides
- state frameworks aligned with the content standards
- national standards for each subject in the curriculum guides
- access to the Internet for retrieving other state resources such as test blueprints
- curriculum materials referenced in the district's curriculum guide

All of these materials needed to be readily accessible to teachers as soon as they completed their professional development program.

After Mrs. Lewis was satisfied that sufficient time and curriculum resources would be available to her teachers, she prepared the school's broader community for the changes on the way. She counted on assistance from respected lead teachers, including Mrs. Hernandez, to help her advocate for the standards with the rest of the staff. The district had anticipated the need for lead teachers' support when it chose to include them in administrator training for the new curriculum management procedures. Now these teachers played a critical role in the district's advocacy program for curriculum change.

The administration understood that teachers wanted to be part of major decisions and to be informed about changes before they happened. Lead teachers thus were encouraged to talk with their colleagues about the training they experienced and to share news about upcoming changes with school staff. The lead teachers served as trusted colleagues who could effectively describe the new roles to be learned in professional development sessions.

As the time for professional development for teachers drew near, lead teachers and administrators described the SAPC as a means for improving student achievement beyond what was possible by merely aligning the curriculum with the standards. Mrs. Hernandez informed her 2nd grade colleagues that the new planning procedures were easy to follow. She told them that teachers would share responsibility for conducting the new planning activities in groups. Most important, she notified the teachers that they would be given a full year to practice the SAPC before instructional supervision would be modified to evaluate standards-based lessons. Mrs. Lewis and Mrs. Hernandez knew that the rank and file of teachers in their school needed to believe that they could perform the SAPC with no undue hardship and that student achievement would improve as a result of teachers' collaborative efforts.

Mrs. Lewis and her lead teachers learned to anticipate teachers' problems. During administrator training, they discovered through their own efforts with the SAPC that translating content statements of the standards and frameworks into vivid descriptions of standards-meeting student performances was the most challenging step in the

SAPC. Mrs. Hernandez and other lead teachers prepared for their new roles as planning coaches who would help grade-level teams with their deliberations. In addition, Mrs. Lewis scheduled biweekly faculty meetings dedicated to resolving problems and concerns with the SAPC during the first six months of the installation process.

Prior to the end of the academic year, Mrs. Lewis was ready to lead her teachers from professional development to a successful installation of the SAPC. She was confident that each of the lead teachers knew how to use the new curriculum guides, how to help teachers in grade-level teams use state standards resources, and how to lead group discussions of student work samples for instructional improvement. Moreover, each lead teacher knew how to augment the curriculum guide for her specific grade level by adding standards-based lessons and exemplary student work samples with teacher commentary to the growing compendium of resources in the curriculum guides.

As the district's teachers began their professional development in the last days of the school year, Mrs. Lewis and the other principals acquired advanced skills in the curriculum management process. These skills included the use of the district's standards assessment system for instructional improvement and augmentation of the classroom observation and supervision process to sustain the SAPC after the installation year was completed.

Supporting a Successful Installation

The professional development program for teachers included two days of activity at the end of the school year and two days right before the start of the next school year. (See Chapter 7 for details.) As districtwide training for elementary school teachers came to a close, all participants were informed that school schedules would accommodate the SAPC beginning with the first week of classes. This expectation for immediate installation of the SAPC following professional development placed a special obligation on school leadership teams to channel the momentum of training into professional practice without interruption.

The Formation of Planning Teams

The teachers were told during their professional development that they would begin SAPC collaboration in grade-level teams on the Wednesday of the first week of school and that planning would be conducted every Wednesday afternoon thereafter. During this first week, Mrs. Lewis held two meetings with Mrs. Hernandez and other grade-level leaders. The first meeting was held Tuesday afternoon and the second on Thursday afternoon. The Tuesday meeting was needed to verify that each planning team was prepared for the first collaborative lesson planning session to be conducted the following day. The Thursday session was needed to receive feedback from team leaders about successes and problems arising from the first round of grade-level meetings. Mrs. Lewis had previously informed her team leaders that weekly meetings would be held through the first 10 weeks of school to make sure the SAPC was getting off to a good start at each grade level.

Biweekly faculty meetings were dedicated to schoolwide sharing of problems and successes with the SAPC. During these meetings, Mrs. Lewis, Mrs. Hernandez, and other team leaders, sometimes with support from district curriculum leaders, conducted continuing professional development in the SAPC to ensure a thorough and complete installation of the new processes for lesson planning and student work evaluation. Topics at these sessions included using district curriculum resources to identify skills and concepts in content statements of the standards and frameworks, writing performance descriptions that function well for evaluating students' work, and using search engines and Internet sites to find information and curriculum resources that could meet lesson objectives.

The team leaders and Mrs. Lewis developed the agenda for each of these faculty meetings in response to concerns raised during SAPC sessions. Teachers' concerns were the priority consideration for the weekly Thursday afternoon sessions of the school leadership council.

The Involvement of the Superintendent

Mrs. Lewis met with Dr. Castro, the district's superintendent, and with the rest of the district's curriculum leadership every week for the first 10 weeks of the SAPC installation. During these sessions, principals described the progress that their schools were making toward regular and effective use of the SAPC. As problems with specific subject matter emerged, district curriculum specialists were delegated to find solutions. If one or two schools experienced particular difficulties, the specialists were assigned to assist the planning teams at those schools.

The SAPC installation process was the centerpiece of districtwide curriculum work for those first months of school. The first district curriculum planning day, held in early November, was dedicated to reinforcing the need for, and value of, standards-based teaching and learning. Teams experiencing success gave testimonials in the morning. In the afternoon, a panel of curriculum experts and lead teachers resolved problems presented by planning teams.

Dr. Castro knew that the district's efforts could go only so far in sustaining teachers' early work with the SAPC. It was up to principals to provide the leadership needed to build and support teacher confidence in the new activities. Mrs. Lewis, one of the more capable principals of the district, was able to meet this expectation.

The Importance of the Principal's Leadership

Mrs. Lewis demonstrated a consistent and abiding interest in the activities of each grade-level team as they met to plan lessons and, later, to evaluate students' work. Mrs. Hernandez and other teachers sensed Mrs. Lewis's commitment to the SAPC when they saw that she was dedicating most of her faculty meeting time to checking on their progress. It was clear to the teachers that the principal understood each of the elements of standards-based teaching and learning, including the essential steps of the SAPC. Casual conversations with Mrs. Lewis always included the principal's questions and concerns about each teacher's progress with the new planning and evaluation activities. She consistently expressed sincere interest in each teacher's questions or concerns about standards-based teaching.

After the new school year was well under way and lead teachers reported that teams were adjusting to the new planning activities, Mrs. Lewis started to make informal visits with planning groups during

Wednesday afternoon SAPC sessions. She took care to drop in when lesson planning was being conducted. She knew that many teachers would be anxious about collaborative evaluation of students' work. Many of them would be comparing the performance of their students with the performance of other teachers' students for the first time. She thus wisely waited for some additional time to pass before she participated in conversations about the quality of students' work.

These informal visits with planning teams served two purposes. First, Mrs. Lewis hoped to reinforce teachers' efforts and to show support for the process. She wanted to understand the challenges that teachers were experiencing. Through these visits, she was able to demonstrate that consistent performance of the SAPC was her highest priority for the school year. Second, she wanted to prepare teachers for the new supervision activities planned for the second year of the installation process. Teachers would be more comfortable with the formal conversations about their lesson plans and student work samples during the upcoming supervision sessions if they held preliminary conversations with the principal in their own classrooms in a nonevaluative manner during the first year of SAPC activity.

The Process of Informing the Community

Successful installation of the SAPC was also supported by outreach efforts to parents and the community. Back-to-school night was dedicated to informing parents about the progress that students were making with standards-based learning. The evening started with a plenary session in the school cafeteria where parents were told about teachers' collaborative planning and work evaluation activities, including close examination of students' work in relation to the expectations of the standards. Then parents visited their children's classrooms, where teachers described their collaborative work with grade-level teams and displayed standards, frameworks, and curriculum resources used in the planning process. Parents were provided with information about the critical standards to be achieved in each subject.

Bulletin boards in classrooms and hallways featured examples of students' work that met the standards. The main office and building entrance featured displays of critical standards to be achieved during the school year. Mrs. Lewis and the teachers informed parents about the school's new focus on standards achievement and the supportive role that parents could play in helping their students produce work that meets the standards. Parents were advised to obtain their own copy of state frameworks from the state department of education Web site or from the school so that they would understand the school's expectations for their children.

Supervising and Sustaining the Planning Cycle

As the first year of new standards implementation continued to unfold, teachers at Mariposa became used to the routines of the SAPC. A new school culture began to emerge. Conversations about the instructional planning process were frequently heard in the teachers' lounge. By December, grade-level teams had already compiled more than seven standards-based lessons and several sets of student work samples.

With the arrival of the second half of the school year, Mrs. Lewis used monthly faculty meetings to introduce revisions to the lesson observation process and postobservation conference protocol that had been successfully negotiated with the teachers' union. All teachers who had a full year of practice with the SAPC would be supervised with this new protocol. Members of the district's instructional leadership team, lead teachers who had been trained with principals, and union leaders were involved in the protocol's development. The protocol included expectations of teachers and administrators during each of three important events in the instructional supervision cycle: preobservation preparations, observation using evaluative criteria, and postobservation procedures and discussions.

The new protocol would apply to collaboratively developed lessons. Other lessons developed by teachers in the course of traditional lesson planning would be evaluated using the district's traditional protocol, which was similar to the supervision cycle found in most public schools. The union and the administration agreed that all observations of collaboratively developed lessons would be announced and scheduled by appointment.

Preobservation Expectations

The administration and the teachers' union agreed that certain requirements should be met before an administrator conducted an observation of a standards-based lesson resulting from SAPC deliberations. They decided that administrators would ask for a copy of the collaboratively developed lesson plan within one week of the scheduled observation. Administrators would provide the expectations for the lesson in the form of a checklist at the time they asked teachers to make an appointment for an observation (see Figure 5.1 on p. 98).

As a result of the negotiated agreements, Mrs. Lewis now expects her teachers to submit a lesson plan before she observes instruction. In evaluating the plan, she looks for each element of a standards-based lesson (presented in Chapter 3). Mrs. Lewis uses the appropriate curriculum guide to check the learning expectations of the selected standards to see whether they represent a reasonable amount of content to be developed within the time allotted. Ideally, no more than three standards should appear in the lesson plan, and they should be edited to reflect the specific objectives of the lesson.

Mrs. Lewis reviews the lesson's objectives, relying on copies of the relevant framework and curriculum guide to make judgments. The objectives should include clear and explicit descriptions of student performances or products and should be written from the content statements of the selected standards. The objectives are active-voice descriptions of products or performances to be demonstrated during the lesson, and they need to include adjectives and qualifying statements that characterize a proficient performance. Some behaviors and products will be generated during class time, but others may result from homework. Mrs. Lewis will not be able to identify proficient student behaviors and performances if the lesson's objectives do not include these characterizations.

The principal also examines the lesson's activities to see whether they are likely to elicit standards-meeting student products and performances. Activities should lead students to demonstrate the behaviors and products described in the objectives. She reviews copies of materials to be distributed to students during the lesson, along with the lesson plan, in order to make this determination.

FIGURE 5.1

Expectations for Standards-Based Lesson Plans

Expectations	Met	Partially Met	Not Met
The lesson topic is related to a selected standard or standards.	❏	❏	❏
Selected standards are identified by subject, grade level, or course and are transcribed from frameworks or other state documents.	❏	❏	❏
Selected standards have been edited and delimited to topics and skills that can be acquired in the lesson that will be observed.	❏	❏	❏
Lesson objectives describe student behaviors or products that will be observable during the lesson or in students' work resulting from the lesson.	❏	❏	❏
Lesson objectives will lead students to demonstrate skills and knowledge described in the standards or content statements of the frameworks.	❏	❏	❏
A sequence of learning activities is provided, and the activities are likely to elicit the performances and products found in the objectives.	❏	❏	❏
Materials to be distributed to students and activities of the lesson will develop the academic vocabulary of the selected standards.	❏	❏	❏
Evaluation methods and materials will elicit performances or products that meet the expectations of the objectives.	❏	❏	❏
Evaluation materials expect students to use and apply academic language of the standards, content statements, and objectives.	❏	❏	❏

Comments:

_____

_____

_____

_____

Mrs. Lewis uses the checklist in Figure 5.1 to conduct the lesson plan assessment. If she finds that some required elements of the plan are not met, she returns the plan to the teacher for revision prior to the observation. If the lesson plan is satisfactory, she confirms the date and time of the observation.

Instructional Supervision

Mrs. Lewis brings several items to the classroom at the time of the lesson observation, including the lesson plan, all student materials to be used during the lesson, a lesson evaluation checklist, and a copy of the curriculum guide used for the planning of the lesson. During the observation, she looks for the elements that are typically assessed in conventional supervisory visits: the engagement of students in lessons, the effective use of transitions between activities, the clarity of the teacher's directions as perceived by students, and the responses of students to the teacher's directions and classroom management procedures. By agreement with the union, Mrs. Lewis and other district supervisors pay additional attention to evidence of standards-based teaching and student achievement by noting such points as

• the teacher's overt statement or posting of the standards to be addressed in the day's lesson

• the presence of student behaviors and products described in the objectives of the lesson

• students' use of academic language found in the content statements of the frameworks, the selected standards of the lesson, and the lesson's objectives

• modifications or additions to printed materials intended to elicit behaviors or products that meet the lesson's objectives

Mrs. Lewis uses a district-approved evaluation form during her observations that was created with lead teachers and union representatives (see Figure 5.2 on p. 100). Its development was highly public and was brought to the attention of teachers for their input. The administration worked to make the expectations noted on the form clear and unambiguous.

FIGURE 5.2

Criteria for Evaluating a Standards-Based Lesson

Criteria	Fully Evident	Partially Evident	Not Evident
Standards posted in the classroom are appropriate and timely for development in accordance with the curriculum pacing guide.	❑	❑	❑
Students are appropriately informed of standards that they are achieving or will achieve.	❑	❑	❑
Assignments and announcements of upcoming student activities relate to standards to be achieved in accordance with the curriculum pacing guide.	❑	❑	❑
Students are appropriately informed of the performance or product expectations before or during the lesson.	❑	❑	❑
The teacher uses, and explains, academic vocabulary of the selected standards during the lesson.	❑	❑	❑
Activities of the lesson unfold as they were described in the lesson plan.	❑	❑	❑
Student performances and products described in the lesson's objectives can result from the learning activities in the lesson plan.	❑	❑	❑
Student performances and products demonstrated during the lesson meet proficiency levels described in the lesson's objectives.	❑	❑	❑
Evaluation activities expect students to provide products or performances that are described in the lesson's objectives.	❑	❑	❑

Comments:

_____

_____

_____

_____

_____

In prior years, Mrs. Lewis focused on a teacher's instructional behaviors and the students' responses to directions. If the lesson plan was followed, then it was judged to have been effective, even if it did not specifically describe what students were to know or be able to do as a result of instruction. By contrast, Mrs. Lewis now evaluates a lesson as successful if students demonstrate the achievement of content and skills identified in the lesson's objectives. In general, a standards-based lesson is likely to be successful if it meets the conditions identified in Figure 5.2 and exhibits the following characteristics:

• The activities of the lesson elicit expected student performances and products described in the objectives of the lesson plan.

• The academic language of the standard is conveyed by the teacher and used properly by students.

• Students' actions result in products and behaviors described in the lesson's objectives.

• The language of the classroom and the nature of the tasks performed by students are on par with the cognitive challenges evident in the selected standards and content statements.

In addition, the following negative indicators should *not* be present in the classroom during the observation:

• large amounts of desk work involving commercial response sheets that do not call for the production of work described in the objectives of the lesson plan

• unchallenging tasks such as matching exercises, sentence completion, word searches, and puzzles

• textbook exercises or end-of-chapter problems that are not related through the lesson's objectives to the standards selected for the lesson

Postobservation Expectations

Following a lesson observation, Mrs. Lewis asks the teacher to select four or five samples of students' work produced during or for the lesson. These samples should reflect the general range of quality found in the work of the entire class. The teacher photocopies each of the selected samples, then processes and returns the originals to students along with the other work submitted by the rest of the class.

The teacher reviews each of the selected work samples, looking for products or performances described in the objectives of the lesson plan. The teacher highlights writing, drawings, or other markings that meet the performance descriptions in the objectives and writes comments stating why these elements meet one or more of the lesson's objectives. After reviewing the work samples, the teacher prepares some concluding notes about the samples that respond to each of the following questions:

- Which lesson objectives were achieved in most of the work samples? What evidence supports this conclusion?

- Which lesson objectives were not achieved in the work samples? What errors or missing elements support this conclusion?

- What changes in the lesson might result in improved achievement of the lesson's objectives?

Mrs. Lewis asks the teacher to make an appointment for a follow-up visit within one week of the observation. The teacher gives Mrs. Lewis the annotated work samples to review prior to this post-observation conference. She needs two or three days before the meeting to review the materials. The teacher's lesson plan, the student work samples with highlighted evidence of standards achievement, and the teacher's notes about the work samples form the basis of the conversation at the postobservation conference.

Postobservation Conferences

At the beginning of the meeting, Mrs. Lewis gives the teacher an opportunity to discuss the lesson. If the lesson deviated from the plan or activities did not unfold as described in the plan, the teacher explains the departures from the intended plan—usually certain behaviors or products—and why they happened.

Mrs. Lewis talks about the lesson plan first because it describes the teacher's intentions for student learning. She brings the conversation to important features of the lesson as she observed it, including student behaviors, and then reviews the student work samples. She uses sets of questions to guide her conversation during the post-observation meeting. First, Mrs. Lewis initiates a discussion of the lesson plan:

• What led you to select the standards that appear in the lesson plan?

• What resources did you use to write the lesson objectives of the plan?

• How do the anticipated behaviors and products of the objectives demonstrate the achievement of the selected standards and other content statements in the frameworks?

• Which activities were specifically intended to elicit student behaviors or products described in the objectives?

• What were the evaluation activities of the lesson, and how did they measure achievement of the objectives?

Next, Mrs. Lewis considers the lesson itself:

• Did the activities unfold as described in the lesson plan?

• What student behaviors demonstrated achievement of one or more of the objectives?

• Which objectives were not met, or only partially met, during the course of the lesson?

Finally, Mrs. Lewis reviews the selected examples of students' work:

• Did the student work samples collectively demonstrate achievement of all or some of the objectives?

• Where is the evidence in the work samples that shows that students achieved one or more of the objectives of the lesson?

• What student behaviors or products demonstrate that students acquired and effectively used the academic language of the standard chosen for the lesson?

• Based on what we see in the students' work, what modifications in the lesson would have led to greater achievement of the lesson's objectives?

• Would you change the objectives or activities of the lesson plan following your review of students' work?

• How might you change the lesson to enhance the achievement of the objectives?

Through this observation process, Mrs. Lewis and other principals of the La Senda School District can monitor student achievement and lead their schools toward continuous instructional improvement.

Leading Your School Toward Standards Achievement

If changes in school culture and curriculum practice are to be effectively installed and sustained, the principal must visibly support and participate in all elements of the change process. Effective advocacy by the principal and revised supervision procedures combine to sustain the SAPC until it becomes the foundation of professional practice in a standards-based school. Principals who are currently in the process of installing standards-based practices are encouraged to use the checklist in Figure 5.3 to evaluate the progress they have made so far.

FIGURE 5.3

Checklist for Leading a Standards-Based School

Progress has been made regarding conditions in the school:

_____ The principal can describe the purpose of each of the following documents and how to obtain them from the state department of education: state standards and frameworks, state test blueprints or test specifications, and state assessment plans for implementation of new standards-based tests.

_____ The principal and teachers inform parents about state standards, particularly the critical ones selected for important subjects at each grade level.

FIGURE 5.3   (continued)

_____ The principal knows the difference between norm-referenced standardized tests and criterion-referenced standards-based tests, and knows the nature of the tests used in the state to evaluate standards achievement.

_____ Essential standards are posted in the principal's office, teachers' lounge, hallways, and classrooms.

_____ Regular meeting times are included in the daily schedule to provide for grade-level or subject-area team meetings.

_____ Teachers have up-to-date textbooks aligned with essential state standards selected by the district.

Progress has been made regarding the classroom observation cycle:

_____ The principal asks to see standards-based lesson plans before observing teaching.

_____ Teachers' lesson plans are expected to include objectives that consist of performance descriptions written from standards.

_____ During lessons, teachers monitor and correct student academic behavior in relation to expectations that they included in their lesson objectives.

_____ During observations, the principal notes student acquisition of academic language found in the standards.

_____ The principal occasionally reviews student work samples to assess standards achievement as described in teachers' lesson plans.

_____ During postobservation conferences, the principal reviews lesson plans with teachers to look for standards-based instructional objectives.

_____ The principal and teachers discuss student work samples during postobservation conferences to assess standards achievement.

_____ During the performance evaluation process, the principal informs teachers of the progress they are making toward the achievement of critical standards.

6

Evaluation of Standards Achievement

In this chapter, we will see how the La Senda School District incorporates three different levels of assessment to guide improvements in curriculum, instructional planning, and teaching practices. These levels of assessment include collaborative classroom-based assessments, district-coordinated benchmark tests, and the state standards tests, which involve the accountability measures of No Child Left Behind. The district uses these three assessment strategies in an integrated manner to monitor student achievement of state content standards. The chapter will also introduce Dr. Williams, the district's director of research and assessment, who provides oversight and coordination of all assessment activities. He brings the results of standards-based assessments to the attention of the school district administration, the principals, and the teachers.

Classroom-Based Assessments

The last thing teachers want to hear these days is a recommendation to do more testing. Across the United States, teachers are protesting state and federal testing requirements, claiming that these tests take too much time away from teaching and learning. In the La Senda schools, however, standards-based teaching proceeds with no more testing than would be found in other school districts.

At Mariposa Elementary School, for example, assessment of an informal nature is embedded in the work that students produce in the classroom. Class work, rather than tests, becomes the primary source of information on student progress toward achievement of the standards. Recall the events of Mrs. Hernandez's class that we envisioned in Chapter 1:

> Mrs. Hernandez organizes and facilitates student-centered learning activities for individuals, pairs, or small groups. Following the video, children work in pairs to sort picture cards into the proper order for a frog's life cycle and a butterfly's life cycle. This activity is intended to achieve the following lesson plan objective: "Given pictures of the life cycle stages of frogs and butterflies, students *will place* them in proper order for each animal." The children identify stage names correctly as the teacher moves among the pairs, listening to their responses. Clearly, students are achieving this objective of the lesson plan.

In Mrs. Hernandez's classroom, descriptions of student performances and products are more than the instructional targets of lessons planned with colleagues during SAPC deliberations. They are the primary evaluation tools she uses to assess her students' work in relation to the expectations of the standards.

Incorporating Assessment into Lesson Planning

The 2nd grade teachers bring student work samples to SAPC sessions and compare them with the performance and product descriptions of that lesson's objectives. Let's refer to Mrs. Hernandez's lesson plan (Figure 1.1) to identify the lesson objectives that will be used for this purpose.

> Given pictures of the life cycle stages of frogs and butterflies, students *will place* them in proper order for each animal.
>
> Students *will list* the life cycle stages of frogs and butterflies in proper order.
>
> In a brief skit about the life of a frog or a butterfly, students *will describe* the features of the life cycle stage they are portraying.
>
> Following a reading of *The Very Hungry Caterpillar,* students *will write* a description of themselves growing up as a frog or a butterfly. They *will use* proper stage names and the academic language of the standards in their description.

For this particular lesson, the first objective calls for students to place pictures of life cycle stages in proper order. The qualifying statement *in proper order* becomes the criterion of a proficient performance when Mrs. Hernandez evaluates her students' work.

During each grade-level or subject-area team meeting, the objectives that teachers write from the standards serve two essential functions. First, they are the targets of instruction for the lessons to be taught. Second, they are tools for evaluating the quality of student responses in relation to the expectations of the standards from which the objectives are derived.

Mrs. Hernandez and her team review their science standards and frameworks during an SAPC session. After they identify content statements that need to be expressed as student performance or product descriptions, they ask themselves some questions:

• What will our students draw, write, label, or describe that shows us that they understand the content statements that we selected from the standards?

• How will we know that their understanding is at a depth that exhibits mastery of the selected standard?

• What behaviors can we expect from our students that will show the application of higher-level reasoning skills expected by the standards?

• What learning activities will elicit student performances that demonstrate the knowledge and skills described in our selected content statements?

This first set of questions expresses the teachers' efforts to write lesson objectives from the standards. Their chief concern is to elicit student performances that meet or exceed the learning expectations of the standards. Their next task is to revisit the statements and adapt them to serve their secondary role as tools for evaluating students' work. Questions that will guide the team's deliberations include:

• What attributes or characteristics of the expected student performance will demonstrate that the performance is truly proficient and meets the selected standard?

• What are the dimensions of the expected student response in terms of order, number, accuracy, detail, or explication that meet the expectations of our standard?

Performance descriptions are transformed into assessment tools through the addition of qualifying statements. The qualifying statements serve as criteria that the teachers use to judge their students' work. The difficulty for teachers in this process is developing a shared vision of a proficient student performance and describing the quality elements of that vision. If we look at the culminating product of the life cycles lesson, we can gain deeper insight into the formulation of a shared vision of a proficient student performance.

As Mrs. Hernandez meets with her colleagues, one of them suggests that the students should write an autobiographical statement from the perspective of growing up as a butterfly or a frog. Perhaps the first teacher suggests that the written statement should be a paragraph. The second teacher, agreeing with the first, includes another criterion of proficiency: The paragraph needs to include specific vocabulary of the life cycle stages in proper sequential order from egg to adult. Mrs. Hernandez agrees with that suggestion, and she recommends that students should properly use other academic language of the standard, including *sequence* and *stage*. Finally, all three teachers agree that students should be directed to state some specific characteristic or property of each of the life cycle stages in their paragraph.

The team now writes the prompt that students will receive before the end of the class period on the life cycles of the butterfly and the frog:

> Please write the story of your life growing up as a frog or a butterfly. You should mention each of the stages your life goes through from beginning to end. Be sure to include some information about each stage that tells it apart from the other stages. You should use the words *stage* and *sequence* in a way that shows you understand the meaning of these words.

The teachers are confident that their students will demonstrate knowledge and understanding of life cycle stages through a satisfactory completion of this exercise.

Mrs. Hernandez and her colleagues finish the activity of writing
performance descriptions by rereading the content statements they
selected from the standards. The team checks that the rigor and intellectual growth expected in the content statements of the standards
matches with the rigor and intellectual challenge in their performance
descriptions. This final exercise assures them that they are meeting
the standards through their teaching and their assessment of resulting student work.

Using Performance Descriptions to Review Students' Work

At Mariposa Elementary School, SAPC sessions usually begin with
an evaluation of student work samples that have been collected by the
teachers in the planning group. These samples are the products of
the lesson that was taught since the prior planning session. After
Mrs. Hernandez and her colleagues teach their lessons on the life
cycle stages of the butterfly and the frog, they collect their students'
work as usual, but they set aside four or five samples that reflect the
cross section of student abilities. They photocopy these selected samples, delete students' names, and personally evaluate each one in relation to the criteria of proficiency that appear in the performance
descriptions of their lesson plans.

The teachers read the biographical statements, writing notes
about the presence or absence of each of the evaluative criteria. For
example, the second element to be evaluated is the list of stage names
that students were expected to write in correct sequential order. If
students were asked to label a diagram of stages properly, then accurate names and spellings will also be expected and evaluated. The
teachers comment on the presence or absence of (1) a description of
each life cycle stage, with the names spelled properly; (2) the appear-
ance of the life cycle stage names in proper order; (3) the presence of
a characteristic or property of each stage; and (4) the proper use of
the words *stage* and *sequence* in some part of the autobiographical
statement.

After the teachers have analyzed their own students' work, they are ready to bring the samples to the next SAPC session to discuss the effectiveness of the lesson that they planned together. It is during these discussions that collegial, professional judgments must be made about the quality of students' work in relation to the expectations of the lesson's objectives and the standards from which they were derived. Teachers consider the following questions:

• Does the quality of the work samples, taken as a whole, suggest that the lesson was effective in eliciting standards-meeting work?

• Were the objectives met at a proficient level?

• Was there a student performance expectation that was not evident, not met, or poorly performed in a preponderance of the work samples?

• If several samples displayed less than a proficient performance with regard to a particular performance expectation, what elements of the lesson may not have been successful in preparing students with the requisite skills and knowledge to meet the expectation?

• What improvements in the lesson might be made that would lead to better performances from students the next time the lesson is taught?

• What subsequent actions are necessary to ensure that most students have reached a level of proficiency before moving on?

When the teachers review their students' work and answer these questions sincerely, they launch a continuous cycle of instructional improvement for the benefit of both current and future students.

Developing Alternative Classroom Assessment Tools

Performance descriptions with high-quality proficiency criteria are the essential tools Mrs. Hernandez and her colleagues use when they evaluate students' work in relation to the expectations of the standards. Grade-level and subject-matter teams may use other tools to evaluate standards achievement in the course of a lesson. These additional tools are developed by teachers as they work together to engage the learning expectations of the standards.

In recent years, teachers in New Jersey and California have been recommending strategies at both the secondary and elementary school levels that tend to fall into two distinct categories: (1) direct engagement with standards citations and (2) use of metacognitive tools such as graphic organizers. Other categories are likely, too, but we'll take a look at these two approaches to illustrate how assessment ideas can evolve when teachers understand the structure and content of their standards documents.

Direct engagement with content and process statements of the standards. At Pacific Heights High School, the high school in the La Senda School District, teachers use other methods of classroom assessment suitable for adolescent learners. A team of physics teachers uses a writing protocol that calls for students to restate the concepts and ideas of the science frameworks into their own words. The teachers use these exercises to check student understanding of complex vocabulary and concepts found in the narrative of the frameworks. Students have their own copies of the standards and frameworks, and they understand the structure and organization of these resources.

In a typical exercise, the physics teachers extract a content statement from the standards and ask groups of students to rewrite portions of the statement in their own words. While students perform this task, the teachers move about their classrooms listening for the use of the academic vocabulary of the selected standard. The teachers use this eavesdropping strategy to assess understanding of the critical vocabulary and of problem-solving concepts. They bring their notes about student language use to their collaborative meetings, where they develop a shared understanding of the particular challenges that students are experiencing with the essential ideas of physics described in the standards.

Use of graphic organizers and multisensory tools to elicit expressions of understanding. At Mariposa Elementary School, knowledge of the standards is often expressed through the use of some organizing dimension such as the chronological, sequential (e.g., the life cycle stages of the butterfly), or spatial (e.g., the relative position of geographic features) orientation of related ideas or concepts. Occasionally, relationships between ideas are hierarchically arranged or related through such graphic organizers as concept maps, outlines, tables, or charts. Mrs. Hernandez and the other 2nd grade teachers help students understand the standards by eliciting relationships between new vocabulary and ideas of the standards and prior knowledge from class work or experience.

Creating Checklists and Rubrics

Soon after teachers began regular deliberations using the SAPC, Mrs. Lewis and other administrators realized that there wasn't enough time for teachers to develop a new assessment tool for every standards-based lesson. Checklists, however, could be prepared relatively quickly and used to evaluate student achievement of lesson objectives. During continuing professional development in standards achievement and assessment, the teachers learned how to create checklists from lesson objectives.

On one occasion, the 2nd grade planning team considered the following history–social science standards (California Department of Education, 2005):

> Students understand the importance of individual action and character and explain how heroes from long ago and the recent past have made a difference in others' lives. (p. 47)

> Students place key events and people of the historical era they are studying in a chronological sequence and within a spatial context; they interpret time lines. (p. 75)[1]

From these standards that pertained to their grade level, the teachers developed two performance-based objectives:

> Each student *will identify* the names, nationalities, and contributions of three scientists who gave rise to our current understanding of modern medicine, chemistry, and the nature of matter and energy.

> Each student *will identify* the time period encompassing the lives of the three scientists and *include* the dates of three major historical events that happened in the same time period.

Then the teachers created a checklist (see Figure 6.1 on p. 114) to measure student recall of essential facts behind these stories of scientific discovery.

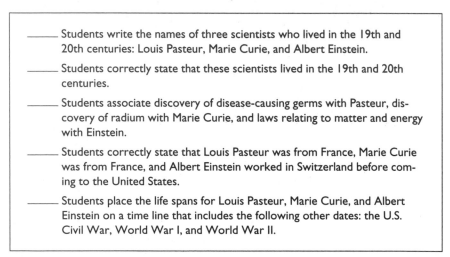

FIGURE 6.1

Checklist for a History of Science Lesson

_____ Students write the names of three scientists who lived in the 19th and 20th centuries: Louis Pasteur, Marie Curie, and Albert Einstein.

_____ Students correctly state that these scientists lived in the 19th and 20th centuries.

_____ Students associate discovery of disease-causing germs with Pasteur, discovery of radium with Marie Curie, and laws relating to matter and energy with Einstein.

_____ Students correctly state that Louis Pasteur was from France, Marie Curie was from France, and Albert Einstein worked in Switzerland before coming to the United States.

_____ Students place the life spans for Louis Pasteur, Marie Curie, and Albert Einstein on a time line that includes the following other dates: the U.S. Civil War, World War I, and World War II.

Mrs. Hernandez and her colleagues had to decide how to use the checklist for evaluating student work samples. Would all five items have to be evident for the work to be deemed proficient? The teachers referred to their history–social science framework and released test items on the California Department of Education Web site to help them reach their decision. In California, history and social science test items seem to be taken from standards statements only. The narrative of the framework is not directly assessed on these state tests. The teachers used this insight to declare only select checklist statements as crucial.

Sometimes teachers at Pacific Heights High School and Mariposa Elementary School prepare analytic rubrics. These evaluation tools are more powerful than checklists because they can be used to identify gradations in the quality of students' work. Typically, rubrics take more time to prepare, so teachers in the La Senda district use them for major projects such as unit reports and papers. Often teachers will distribute rubrics to their students at the time they give the assignment. When students receive a rubric to be used in grading, they learn the quality factors that their teachers expect to find in their work.

When using classroom-based assessments, the teachers in the La Senda School District also consider students with special needs and the alternative means with which they may best express their knowledge and skills. Mrs. Hernandez, for example, extends time limits and offers repeated trials to these students to ensure that they will be able to demonstrate the skills and knowledge of the standards.

At Mariposa, the teachers use the classroom-based standards assessment methods described above to continuously evaluate the everyday progress of instruction. The process of planning lessons during SAPC sessions is coupled with the process of developing assessments. When Mrs. Hernandez envisions a student performance that meets a selected content or process statement of the standards, she also envisions the criteria of proficiency that measure a standards-meeting performance. Her team may choose to assess student learning by directly applying the performance descriptions to student work samples, or they may choose to develop a graphic organizer, checklist, rubric, or other prompt to assess student understanding during the course of a lesson. In any case, standards-based teaching is evident when continuous assessment of standards achievement is built into the classroom routine.

District-Coordinated Benchmark Assessments

The La Senda School District agenda for standards-based reform introduced in Chapter 4 and presented in Figure 4.1 included a sixth and final item: "Develop a coherent system of assessments that measures standards achievement without imposing more test time on teachers and students." A well-designed benchmark-testing program complements the daily assessment of the standards and collaborative evaluation of students' work. The district's teachers can replace some unit and semester exams with the benchmark tests. This decision allows teachers to incorporate standards assessment into the classroom routine and avoid allocating additional days to assessment.

Dr. Williams, the research and assessment director for the district, uses the results of benchmark testing to inform students, parents, teachers, and principals of the progress that students are making toward standards achievement. Through this program, teachers and students know how they are progressing with critical standards likely to be tested on the high-stakes standards exams. Dr. Williams worked with his colleagues to develop a model benchmark-testing program that would prepare teachers and students for the California Standards Tests administered each spring.

Classroom teachers, resource teachers, and curriculum leaders in the La Senda schools spend several days in early August analyzing the standards, frameworks, state-released test items, results from prior state testing, and test blueprints to identify critical standards that contribute coherence to the curriculum and are likely to be tested in the following spring. Teachers use the testing resources to accomplish several goals before the start of the school year.

Updating the Curriculum Guide

A key goal is to update the district's curriculum guides with pacing information for the achievement of critical standards. In the La Senda School District, the academic year is segmented into four intervals for benchmark testing, culminating in the administration of state exams in the spring. The curriculum guides indicate the standards to be covered in each of the four segments, the order in which they should be developed, and the approximate amount of time to be allocated for the development of each standard. Annual adjustments will need to be made to pacing information based on the ability of teachers to convey the curriculum within estimated time intervals. Moreover, information about which standards are tested becomes available with each administration of high-stakes tests. By using the curriculum guides for instructional planning, teachers can lead their students to the achievement of the complete set of standards to be assessed at the end of each segment.

Writing Benchmark Test Items

After the critical standards are identified, sequenced, and placed into the four testing intervals leading up to the state tests in the spring, teachers write test items for each of the critical standards. They try to match the level of challenge, item format, and content distribution likely to appear on the next state tests. This gives the administration a pool of test items to be scheduled into benchmark tests.

During the academic year, Dr. Williams works with lead teachers from all the schools in the district to select test items that reflect the standards to be assessed in each of the four intervals. Typically, 20 items are selected so that the benchmark exams may be completed in a normal instructional period within the block schedule at Pacific Heights High School. Children at Mariposa receive shorter tests with fewer items. The La Senda district uses a commonly available scoring machine that permits each student's response sheet to be coded with identifying information required by state and No Child Left Behind regulations. This coding feature leads to useful disaggregation of test results, allowing the district to follow the progress of learning by student groups of interest. Benchmark test reports are sent to each teacher's computer terminal within 48 hours of test administration. Students and parents receive printed copies of test results shortly thereafter.

Analyzing Benchmark Test Results

Under the leadership of Dr. Williams, the La Senda schools developed a sophisticated system for reporting benchmark scores. Students, parents, teachers, and principals are provided with an organized report that includes useful information for each of these stakeholders in the assessment process (see Figure 6.2 on p. 118). The report indicates (1) each response that was correct or incorrect, (2) the particular standard assessed by each test item, (3) the number and percentage of correct items attributed to each standard taught within the interval assessed by the benchmark test, and (4) the student performance level for all items and standards included on the test.

In Figure 6.2, the student scored 16 correct answers out of 40, resulting in a "below basic" level of performance. The bottom of the report describes the student's performance in relation to each standard. The student performed at a relatively high level with standards associated with writing strategies. Concerns are apparent in other areas, however, notably word analysis, fluency, and systematic vocabulary development.

Figure 6.3 (on p. 120) shows the corresponding test report given to the classroom teacher. This report is a useful tool for improving

FIGURE 6.2

Student Benchmark Test Report

Benchmark Test 3: English/Language Arts

Test Date: 12/02   Grade: 9
School Name: Pacific Heights H. S.   Teacher: Carrillo, Frida
Student: 919191—Vigil, Carol   Period: 3

Question	Standard	Student Response	Question	Standard	Student Response
1	R1.1	B	21	R2.8	A
2	R2.1	A*	22	R2.1	C
3	R2.8	C*	23	R3.9	C
4	R2.4	A	24	R1.1	D
5	R2.4	B*	25	R3.9	B*
6	R1.1	A	26	R3.6	A
7	R2.1	–	27	R3.6	A*
8	R3.9	A*	28	R3.3	A
9	R3.9	A	29	R3.9	B
10	R3.3	B	30	R3.6	D
11	R3.9	C*	31	C1.3	C*
12	R3.6	A*	32	C1.3	A*
13	R3.9	A*	33	W1.9	A*
14	R3.3	A	34	W1.9	A
15	R3.3	D	35	C1.3	B
16	R3.6	B	36	C1.3	C
17	R1.1	B*	37	C1.3	D
18	R2.4	A	38	W1.9	B*
19	R2.4	D	39	C1.3	C*
20	R2.8	C*	40	C1.3	D

Total Correct: 16   % Correct: 40%   * = Correct Response

FIGURE 6.2 (continued)

Student Performance Level				
Far Below Basic	Below Basic	Basic	Proficient	Advanced

◆

Standard	# of Items	# Correct	% Correct
Word Analysis, Fluency, and Systematic Vocabulary Development	4	1	25%
1.1—Identify and use literal and figurative meanings	4	1	
Reading, Comprehension	10	4	40%
2.1—Analyze the structure and format of documents	3	1	
2.4—Synthesize the content; paraphrase ideas	4	1	
2.8—Evaluate the credibility of an author's argument	3	2	
Literary Response Analysis	16	6	38%
3.3—Analyze interactions between characters	4	0	
3.6—Analyze author's development of time; literary devices	5	2	
3.9—Explain how voice and narrator affect characterization, plot	7	4	
Writing Strategies	3	2	67%
1.9—Revise writing to improve organization and word choice	3	2	
Written and Oral English Language Conventions	7	3	43%
1.3—Demonstrate proper English usage and grammar	7	3	

Courtesy of Bob Martinez, Salinas Union High School District.

FIGURE 6.3

Classroom Benchmark Test Report

Benchmark Test 3: English/Language Arts

Test Date:	12/02	
School Name:	Pacific Heights H. S.	
# of Students:	20	

Grade:	9	
Teacher:	Carrillo, Frida	
Period:	3	

Question	Standard	Frequency of Response				Question	Standard	Frequency of Response			
		A	B	C	D			A	B	C	D
1	RI.1	4	1	15	0*	21	R2.8	14	1	2	2*
2	R2.1	19*	0	1	0	22	R2.1	6	5	9	0*
3	R2.8	0	6	13*	1	23	R3.9	2	4	14	0*
4	R2.4	5	10	4	1*	24	RI.1	9	0	0*	11
5	R2.4	3	7*	10	0	25	R3.9	1	11*	3	5
6	RI.1	20	0*	0	0	26	R3.6	19	0	0*	1
7	R2.1	3*	4	2	10	27	R3.6	7*	13	0	0
8	R3.9	5*	5	5	5	28	R3.3	20	0*	0	0
9	R3.9	9	1	8	2*	29	R3.9	5	15	0*	0
10	R3.3	0	4	16	0*	30	R3.6	0*	0	1	19
11	R3.9	1	7	2*	10	31	C1.3	5	8	7*	0
12	R3.6	9*	9	2	0	32	C1.3	4*	0	0	16
13	R3.9	15*	1	2	2	33	W1.9	20*	0	0	0
14	R3.3	17	0	3*	0	34	W1.9	14	2	2	2*
15	R3.3	6*	4	0	10	35	C1.3	6	5	9	0*
16	R3.6	1	19	0	0*	36	C1.3	2	4	14	0*
17	RI.1	7	8*	5	0	37	C1.3	9	0	0*	11
18	R2.4	20	0*	0	0	38	W1.9	1	11*	3	5
19	R2.4	5	1*	4	10	39	C1.3	5	8	7*	0
20	R2.8	3	0	7*	10	40	C1.3	5*	5	5	5

Classroom Total Correct: 177   **Classroom % Correct:** 22%   * = Correct Response

FIGURE 6.3   (continued)

Student Performance Level				
Far Below Basic	Below Basic	Basic	Proficient	Advanced
7	6	2	4	1

Standard	Classroom # of Items	Classroom # Correct	Classroom % Correct
Word Analysis, Fluency, and Systematic Vocabulary Development	80	8	10%
1.1—Identify and use literal and figurative meanings	80	8	
Reading, Comprehension	200	53	27%
2.1—Analyze the structure and format of documents	60	22	
2.4—Synthesize the content; paraphrase ideas	80	9	
2.8—Evaluate the credibility of an author's argument	60	22	
Literary Response Analysis	320	60	19%
3.3—Analyze interactions between characters	80	9	
3.6—Analyze author's development of time; literary devices	100	16	
3.9—Explain how voice and narrator affect characterization, plot	140	35	
Writing Strategies	60	33	55%
1.9—Revise writing to improve organization and word choice	60	33	
Written and Oral English Language Conventions	140	23	16%
1.3—Demonstrate proper English usage and grammar	140	23	

Courtesy of Bob Martinez, Salinas Union High School District.

instruction because it reveals patterns of student responses for the entire class of 20 students.

The classroom report provides the number of responses for each alternative answer to the 40 multiple-choice test questions. We can see that no student selected the correct choice, D, on the first question, which assessed standard R1.1, "Identify and use literal and figurative meanings." By contrast, 13 of the 20 students selected the correct item, C, for the third question, which measured standard R2.8, "Evaluate the credibility of an author's argument." Clearly, the teacher receiving this report would want to know why no students selected the correct answer for the first question.

The report also provides the distribution of student performances across all the standards assessed. Unfortunately, 13 of the 20 students scored either below basic or far below basic. Only five students achieved or surpassed a proficient performance level. This classroom test report leads us ultimately to some key questions. Did the teacher manage to convey the skills and knowledge of all the tested standards within the interval of time covered by the test? What reasons might the teacher provide for the particularly poor performance on standards R1.1 and C1.3? Most important, how will the information on this classroom report be used to improve student understanding of the knowledge it assessed? How will the teacher raise student performances to the basic, proficient, and advanced levels?

Student, classroom, and school reports from the standards-based benchmark exams provide stakeholders with almost immediate feedback concerning progress with the standards. Teachers and administrators can use this information to improve student performance with the standards.

Improving Instruction and Guiding Intervention

Benchmark tests of the kind used in the La Senda School District provide a perfect complement to the state tests administered once a year (discussed later in this chapter). Typically, high-stakes state tests are administered near the end of the school year. Results from the tests might have some value for the following year, but they arrive too late to help students with the content that was tested. By contrast, benchmark tests administered three or four times a year provide information about student understanding that can be used to help achieve important standards before the high-stakes tests. Benchmark tests measure the district's adopted curriculum more precisely, and their timing allows teachers to make adjustments before the state standards tests are administered.

At Mariposa Elementary School, test outcomes are used to validate judgments teachers make about students' work. If test results match the high quality of classroom work seen during SAPC sessions, then instruction proceeds as described in the district's curriculum guide. If, on the other hand, benchmark test results are lower than expected, then teachers may need to adjust their plans in order to enhance student readiness for the high-stakes tests.

In the La Senda schools, teachers and administrators take measures to improve student performances when benchmark tests produce disappointing results. At Mariposa, grade-level teams review their lesson plans and student work products relating to those standards that were not achieved on the benchmark tests. This review may result in revised instructional activities and changed expectations for student products described in lesson objectives. If the review fails to demonstrate reasons for poor student test performance, the teachers may consider other strategies.

At Pacific Heights High School, students who perform poorly on benchmark tests are diverted to supplemental instruction in the form of tutorials and supplemental classes. The high school staff believes in theories of mastery learning that prescribe more instructional time, small-group sessions, and tutorials for students who have not performed well. The school schedule is actually planned to accommodate more instructional time for students who have trouble achieving the standards.

Evaluating the District's Curriculum Management System

Curriculum management for standards achievement brings together several disparate elements into a coherent system of services and resources that support the SAPC. When successfully used by teachers, the SAPC translates content statements of the selected standards into student performance outcomes that meet the standards. The elements of the curriculum management system that are central to this process have been discussed in Chapters 2 and 4, namely the selection of critical standards that are assessed on state tests, the revision of the district's curriculum to include the scope and sequence of the selected standards, the selection of curriculum resources, the modification of the schedule to support the SAPC, and the production of lessons that raise expectations for student learning to meet the selected standards.

Benchmark tests are intended to measure student achievement of the selected critical standards, but they also serve as the most valid measure of the results of the curriculum management system. In addition, they are designed to correlate with state standards tests, which are the ultimate measure of the entire system's success.

State Standards Tests

Curriculum management for standards achievement holds the promise of raising expectations for student learning to achieve many goals. The most valuable goal is to improve the lives and opportunities of students. A more immediate and federally imposed goal for a school district is to improve student achievement on state standards tests tied to the state accountability system, where it exists, and to avoid sanctions stipulated by No Child Left Behind regulations. Therefore, the definitive measure of a successful implementation of the district's curriculum management system is the district's performance on the high-stakes tests used for No Child Left Behind compliance.

Unfortunately, state testing programs vary in the extent to which their high-stakes tests actually reflect the standards. In some states, a publishing company's standardized test is augmented with additional items that assess critical standards. In other instances, specific items of a standardized test are deemed to be "aligned" with state standards, and test results for these particular items are used to report student achievement of state standards. In these states, it is important that a school district's assessment officer understand which components of the state's testing program measure the state's standards and which serve merely as a norm-referenced determination of general student academic learning. Only those components of the state testing system that are aligned with the standards can serve as measures of student standards achievement.

Monitoring Annual Standards Achievement

Student achievement on standards-based tests is only part of adequate yearly progress expected by No Child Left Behind. Other factors, including student participation rates on major tests, contribute to its measure. The component that is most important to the curriculum management process is the achievement of annual measurable objectives on standards-based tests of core subjects, identified by the state and approved by the federal government. Annual measurable objectives are set for key constituencies of school districts, including student groups identified by ethnicity, socioeconomic status, disability, and English-language understanding. School districts are required to disaggregate standards-based test scores to assess the achievement of annual measurable objectives for these important student groups. Test analysis software has become widely available to help districts meet this reporting requirement.

The district can also use the disaggregated test reports to identify the success of its curriculum management system. The information will be most effectively used if it is placed in the hands of teachers in a format that is meaningful to them.

Reviewing the District's Assessment Program

The La Senda School District administration devotes considerable attention to the test results of the prior academic year. Dr. Williams uses commercially available software to display student achievement reports for particular subjects and student groups. These reports are meaningful to the extent that they show student achievement data for district-selected content standards. Dr. Williams and his staff use the summer to accomplish three important tasks.

The first task is to interpret state standards test reports to fulfill external reporting requirements. Through this exercise, the district achieves compliance with state and federal reporting requirements and comes to understand the achievement goals that it must reach to avoid sanctions. Although this function is important with respect to the district's relationship to the state and the need to avoid the political and economic consequences of sanctions, it does not contribute in any substantial sense to the curriculum management process or to the improvement of instruction in the La Senda schools.

The second exercise involves the interpretation of state test results into meaningful information for principals, teachers, and community members. In other states, test disaggregation and analysis for the assessment of standards achievement depends on the kind of examinations used in the state. Some states use norm-referenced standardized tests to measure standards achievement. Typically, the state matches specific examination items on the standardized tests to particular standards, and then reports standards achievement based on student performance on these selected items. If we want to see how students are performing on critical standards, we will need to see reports that describe the achievement of our students in relation to criteria that correspond to a proficient performance on given standards. States using norm-referenced exams to measure standards achievement must determine whether students meet proficiency criteria on each of the standards the tests are designed to measure.

If a state uses a criterion-referenced exam developed expressly to assess student achievement of the state's standards, then the process of extracting meaningful results from the test is made easy by the fact that all test items are linked to the standards. In California, students are reported as "far below basic," "below basic," "basic," "proficient," and "advanced." Only proficient and advanced performances are acceptable. Performance task outcomes or multiple-choice results that are scored as proficient or advanced should be equivalent in rigor to the performance expectations of standards-based lesson objectives and benchmark assessments. Scores in the ranges of far below basic, below basic, and basic indicate that students are not meeting expectations on the same standards assessed in their classroom work products or benchmark tests. These scores will also be shared with the teachers who were responsible for the achievement of each critical standard.

As summer draws to a close, Dr. Williams and other staff members tackle their third task: preparing reports on student achievement for school administrators and teachers. Achievement reports concerning the prior year's students are used to identify challenges for the upcoming year's students. When student performance on selected standards falls below expectations, the teachers at Mariposa Elementary School and Pacific Heights High School review instruction of these particular standards. Occasionally, the curriculum pacing guide is adjusted to give more time to the development of skills and knowledge of a particular standard. Mrs. Hernandez and other lead teachers at Mariposa work together before the start of the school year to write benchmark test items and reschedule the achievement of standards for the upcoming year. They use the results of the prior year's standards tests to develop an effective strategy for standards achievement in the subsequent year.

The performance of the aforementioned three tasks enables the district to obtain the maximum value possible from the spring test results. All affected parties are informed of the test outcomes, and the educators of the district use the state test results to make important adjustments to the curriculum. In addition, this process confirms the accuracy of the district's two other approaches to standards assessment: evaluation of student work samples as part of the SAPC and administration of districtwide benchmark tests.

Comprehensive Standards Assessment in Your School

Through thoughtful planning and collaboration, the administration of the La Senda district was able to install three types of assessment for standards achievement that complemented one another: collaborative evaluation of students' work, benchmark testing, and analysis of state standards tests. As a result, the district was able to effectively assess student progress toward standards achievement and continually improve the quality of the curriculum. School leaders may want to use the checklist in Figure 6.4 (on p. 128) to compare their assessment system with that of the La Senda schools.

FIGURE 6.4

Checklist for a District Standards Assessment System

Assessment is included in planning activities:

_____ Teachers plan lessons that lead students to exhibit standards-meeting products or behaviors during the course of instruction.

_____ Lesson plans include objectives that clearly identify the products or behaviors students must exhibit to meet selected state standards.

_____ During planning sessions, teachers agree on quality criteria that should be evident in student work samples.

_____ Teachers identify the academic vocabulary of the standards that students should use in the course of the lesson.

Assessment is conducted in group sessions:

_____ Teachers use lesson objectives to evaluate students' work that results from daily teaching.

_____ Teachers meet regularly to exchange student work samples and collaboratively evaluate student performances.

_____ Teachers modify lesson plans after they are taught when evidence in students' work suggests the need for changes.

_____ Teachers prepare checklists that use proficiency criteria to evaluate students' work in relation to learning expectations in lesson objectives.

_____ Teachers write checklists and rubrics for major assignments.

_____ Rubrics clearly identify quality criteria that characterize standards-meeting performances expected in major projects.

A benchmark-testing program has been developed:

_____ Teachers and curriculum leaders work together to develop benchmark test items.

_____ Standards, frameworks, state test blueprints, and state-released test items are used to write benchmark test items.

_____ Benchmark tests are administered three or four times a year, and they are constructed from the test item pool developed by teachers and curriculum leaders.

_____ Benchmark test results are provided to students, teachers, principals, and district curriculum leaders.

_____ Teachers are trained to use benchmark test results to identify district-selected standards in need of attention.

_____ Teachers use benchmark test results and classroom assessment results to improve lessons.

FIGURE 6.4   (continued)

State test results are analyzed:

_____ Lead teachers, principals, and other school leaders understand how the state testing system measures the achievement of district-selected state standards.

_____ The district assessment coordinator interprets state test results for ease of consumption by school leaders and teachers.

_____ Teachers receive district reports on state test results and can use them to evaluate student performances on standards for which teachers are held accountable.

_____ Lead teachers and curriculum leaders compare results on the benchmark tests and the state standards exams to enhance alignment between the benchmark-testing program and the state testing program.

_____ Lead teachers and curriculum leaders know how to interpret classroom assessment, benchmark test results, and state standards test results to improve the curriculum planning process by teacher planning teams.

7

Professional Development for Standards Achievement

When the superintendent and other leaders of the La Senda School District realized the complexity of their reform commitment, they planned for professional development at all tiers of the district, including at the building and classroom levels. Unfortunately, professional development in education is often equated with teacher training. Dr. Castro knew this limited perspective would not help the district implement broad-based change in curriculum and teaching practices required for standards achievement. The La Senda leaders had to develop a shared vision of standards achievement in the district's schools.

This vision entailed acceptance of new curriculum policies that focused on instructional planning and teaching. Once the policies were in place, strategic planning was designed to enact the policy changes. The strategic plan included a professional development component to prepare administrators and teachers for their new roles and responsibilities. District leaders, including board of education members, needed to learn their roles in the new policy environment designed for standards achievement. A comprehensive professional development program was planned for Mrs. Lewis, Mrs. Hernandez, and other school leaders. These individuals would function as mentors, coaches, and guides for classroom teachers as they began to apply the new lesson planning and student work evaluation protocol.

The success or failure of the entire change process depended on the dispositions of teachers toward their responsibilities in standards-based teaching and learning. Through the professional development program, they acquired new skills and information that affected their daily responsibilities. The priority topics in the training sessions included

• the use of new curriculum resources for standards-based instructional planning

• the role of each teacher as a collaborating professional when conducting the SAPC

• the development of assessment procedures to analyze student products

• the interpretation of benchmark test results to guide changes in instruction

In this chapter, we will review the characteristics of all the professional development programs for the La Senda district. We will begin by examining the program for district leaders as it was planned under Dr. Castro's leadership.

Designing a District Leadership Program

Dr. Castro anticipated the need for professional development for school board members and central office personnel prior to the installation of a standards-based curriculum in the La Senda schools. Although board members would not actually perform the new routines and procedures of standards-based reforms, they would be approving all expenses and personnel changes that are a part of the reform process. As representatives of their community, the board members needed to be advocates for curriculum reform and standards achievement. They would also monitor the success of the standards-based reform program and support needed changes to keep student achievement gains on track. For these reasons, Dr. Castro made the decision to work on the design of the professional development program for the district leaders before working on programs for principals and teachers.

Integrating Principles of Adult Learning

Dr. Castro and his staff called on the principles of adult education to design the professional development program for the La Senda leadership team. They incorporated some time-honored strategies into the training program:

• Relate knowledge and skills of the program to the professional's current responsibilities and activities.

• Describe new knowledge and skills in terms of actions or decisions that the professional usually makes.

• Illustrate ideas and principles with practical applications likely to develop in the implementation process.

• Show the relationship of new skills and ideas to the systemic change process in the organization.

• Focus instruction on the learner, with opportunities to practice new skills in a supported, collaborative process.

• Acknowledge the learner's existing skills and experience and relate the new skills and activities to them.

Preparing the Leadership for Change

The superintendent met with his staff to review their understanding of state policies and regulations relating to standards-based reforms. They discussed their knowledge of successful efforts by other school districts working with the standards mandate. These meetings led to the identification of outcomes for the district that would be achieved through its leadership development program. The central outcome was board member support and advocacy for standards-based reforms, including the SAPC as the central mechanism for standards achievement.

Following the staff meetings, Dr. Castro met with the president of the La Senda Board of Education to describe a vision of district reorganization for standards achievement. He was elated when the president suggested that a weekend retreat for all members of the board would be a good start for the change process. Dr. Castro and the central office staff began preparations for the retreat by drawing up a list of policy statements for consideration by the board members. The staff brainstormed the following policy statements from research and practice in standards-based teaching and learning:

• The state standards are the primary tools for setting instructional targets for the students of the school district. The achievement of state standards by all students is an essential purpose of the curriculum.

• Teachers must have structured, collaborative planning time in the course of the school day to develop standards-based lessons and evaluate their effectiveness.

• The effective performance of tasks within the SAPC will lead to student achievement goals that are important to the district.

• All teachers and supervisors must have standards-based planning resources readily available. These include print resources, Internet access, opportunities to collaborate, and time for planning.

• Principals and other school leaders have a primary responsibility for providing the enabling conditions and support systems that teachers need to implement standards-based teaching and learning as daily practice.

Dr. Castro considered a number of different retreat activities that would apply principles of adult learning theory to the achievement of consensus on the policy statements. The retreat would start with general discussion on the need for reform, continue with analysis of studies related specifically to the proposed policy statements, and end with recommendations and suggestions to guide the district's leaders through strategic planning and organized committee work. The first activity of the retreat would be a Socratic seminar organized around a shared reading experience.

Dr. Castro invited members of the board of education and his leadership team to read an important article on an element of the anticipated reform effort. He selected an essay that offered guidance on the implementation of standards-based education in public schools.[1]

The superintendent engaged the services of a facilitator to guide participants through the Socratic seminar, which allowed him and his colleagues to participate in the exercise themselves. The facilitator asked open-ended questions about educational reform as it related to the selected article and to current conditions within the La Senda schools. The seminar helped participants understand their colleagues' opinions and concerns about the reform process that was to unfold in the district. It provided clarification of the essential values that team leaders would need to embrace as a prerequisite to strategic planning.

Moving from Policy to Strategy

Once the leaders understood the core beliefs underlying proposed district changes in curriculum and teaching, the facilitator suggested a second conversation that focused on specific practices to be included in the new curriculum management model for the La Senda schools. During this exercise, district leaders considered research reports and policy studies and their implications for standards achievement. Proposals for the curriculum change process described in the selected article were presented and explored for possible adaptation by the district.[2]

A facilitated discussion of successful reform strategies and experiences at other school districts helped the leaders craft a vision of practices and outcomes in a standards-achieving district. The next stage called for a strategic plan for implementing the new program, beginning with the creation of an action agenda to frame the planning process (see Figure 4.1). A committee structure, described in Chapter 4, guided the development of each element of the new system in keeping with the district's vision.

Developing a Shared Vision of Reform

Dr. Castro and the president of the board of education chose to pursue planning through a weekend retreat. Other approaches would have worked as well. Key district leaders and board members could have attended a conference focusing on effective practices in a standards-based environment. Appropriate themes for a conference may include learning communities, performance-based instruction, curriculum standards, or strategic planning. Following the conference, district leaders could discuss other topics in a seminar similar in nature to the Socratic seminar described above.

The mechanism used to bring leaders together is less important than the goals to be achieved. Through effective planning and constructive communication, district leaders can reach a consensus on the essential changes needed for standards achievement. Once the leaders have agreed on a vision for standards-based teaching and learning, the strategic plan will guide them through capacity-building exercises and pave the way for professional development for all the district's teachers.

Creating Effective Professional Development

During the last decade, researchers have actively investigated the factors that contribute to effective professional development programs. Guskey (2003) and Sparks (Guskey & Sparks, 2002), for instance, have studied promising features of professional development programs that lead to changes in classroom practices. Their task has been difficult because few studies have demonstrated causal connections between teacher training and student learning. Nevertheless, the research points to a number of quality elements in professional development programs.

Teachers tend to see merit in programs that connect new pedagogical and content knowledge to their current teaching responsibilities. Clearly, teachers are going to be attracted to the ideas of people who can help them perform their jobs in more effective ways. New ideas, however, are not enough. Teachers need opportunities to practice new skills and methods in a sheltered or coached environment that is similar to, or actually includes, their classrooms. New skills are more likely to be included in teaching when specific directions for their use and additional planning time are included in the program. Single-session workshops offered in hotel conference rooms are simply not an effective format for producing sustained change in teaching behaviors.

Teachers generally enjoy collegiality and professional interaction during training activities, but they may find collaborative planning and student work evaluation threatening when first used with peers back in the workplace. Teachers typically plan their lessons and evaluate students' work in isolation. Professional development programs that expect teachers to collaborate in these activities will need to include provisions for building and sustaining trust between colleagues.

Two other characteristics of effective professional development relate to persistence of effort with new teaching practices. New skills are likely to be applied in classrooms when teachers share responsibility for their implementation and see their colleagues experiencing success. Additionally, the faculty of a school will persist with novel approaches to teaching if the principal expects to see new behaviors learned in professional development, and if coaching, supportive feedback, and encouragement guide initial efforts. In the long term, teachers will continue with a practice only if they see inherent value in their new skills and only if they are internally motivated to continue with them. Internal motivation emerges when teachers believe that they (1) will improve student learning by applying the skills learned in the professional development program; (2) will be able to perform their new tasks and responsibilities successfully without undue burden; and (3) will not suffer consequences, including embarrassment, for difficulties that arise during early attempts with the new skills.

In summary, a positive attitude about new skills is more likely to emerge when training includes the practical application of these skills in practicum settings that emulate real classroom conditions. Teachers are more likely to try new skills in classrooms if they have seen their colleagues performing them with relative ease during initial training experiences. They are more likely to continue using these skills when they work together to sustain implementation efforts rather than working in isolation.

Initiating Professional Development for Leaders

Dr. Castro knew from the early days of the district's planning process that principals and lead teachers would serve as catalysts for expected changes in lesson planning and instruction. Their commitment to the SAPC and their knowledge of its elements would lead to teacher persistence with the protocol during the crucial first year of practice. Teachers will sense their principal's commitment when they believe that she fully understands the elements of standards-based teaching and learning, including the essential steps of the SAPC. For these reasons, Mrs. Lewis and other principals of the La Senda School District received thorough training in the SAPC and the supporting role they would play in the curriculum management system before teachers were trained. Mrs. Hernandez and other lead teachers were included in the leadership training so they could help communicate the benefits of the system to the rest of the teaching staff.

Mrs. Lewis learned how to advocate for reform, support reform practices in the classroom, provide her staff with standards-based instructional resources, and supervise standards-based instruction. In addition, Mrs. Hernandez and other lead teachers played key supporting roles in nurturing and encouraging collaborative planning teams as they started to use the SAPC following initial training.

Advocating for Reform

As described in Chapter 5, Mrs. Lewis learned how to demonstrate her commitment to the change process and how to support teachers' early efforts with the SAPC. She advocated for the district's reform strategies through a variety of means, including modeling, role playing, and scenario analyses. Principals can convey the importance of standards implementation to teachers by

• conducting classroom walkthroughs to identify specific standards-meeting behavior of students, followed by communicating with teachers to encourage standards-based teaching practices;

• visiting collaborative planning groups during their SAPC sessions in an unobtrusive, nonthreatening manner;

• planning agendas for back-to-school nights and keeping parents informed about changes under way at the school;

• highlighting critical standards in the main office, teachers' lounge, and other congregating areas; and

• conducting faculty meetings that support the reform process.

Supporting Classroom Efforts

In the La Senda district, lead teachers were pivotal to the success of the entire reform enterprise, especially during the early days of standards implementation. They met with the classroom teachers to guide them through their first efforts with the SAPC. Younger, less experienced teachers expressed some frustration with the new tasks of standards-based planning and student work evaluation. Additionally, some senior teachers who had always been comfortable with their professional isolation were reluctant to participate in collaborative planning and student work evaluation activities. Mrs. Hernandez and other lead teachers at Mariposa Elementary School demonstrated tact, technical assistance, and encouragement during collaborative planning sessions.

The lead teachers learned their important advocacy responsibilities during professional development with the principals. Their training included discussion of anticipated resistance behaviors, problem-solving scenarios for planning sessions, and modeling of appropriate means to communicate support and provide technical assistance during collaborative planning. The principals and lead teachers learned to accept the inevitable concern and anxiety that surface when collaborative planning and student work evaluation begin in the schools.

Providing Instructional Resources

During their professional development, Mrs. Lewis and Mrs. Hernandez became acquainted with the complete inventory of standards planning resources that would be allocated to the teachers at Mariposa. They needed to get standards, frameworks, adopted materials, blueprints, and any other tools into the hands of teachers in an efficient and cost-effective manner. Mrs. Hernandez learned the content and organization of the resources for her grade level and how to use them for planning and work evaluation purposes. Each lead teacher was assigned a specific group of teachers to coach through the steps of the SAPC.

The teachers would need specific standards materials for their lesson planning and student work evaluation activities. For example, the 3rd grade team leader reviewed the resources for the core subjects taught at his grade level and found that the history–social science frameworks are formatted differently than the math frameworks. He would need to show his team how the materials are organized and how they can be used as references during the planning process. The professional development for lead teachers focused on close examination and understanding of the instructional resources and ways to share this information with colleagues.

Supervising Standards-Based Planning

All the lead teachers worked as members of at least one planning team. Their deep involvement in each step of the SAPC and their leadership ensured a good start with new collaborative planning methods. These early successes resulted from their expert knowledge with the most challenging steps of the SAPC and their ability to foster the development of trust and honest disclosure within planning groups.

Lead teachers' expertise in standards-based planning came from two exposures to the SAPC. The first occurred during training with principals in a three-day professional development workshop. The agenda for principal and lead teacher training is included in Figure 7.1 (on p. 140). During the three-day workshop, principals and lead teachers identified content statements and learning expectations from state standards resources. They learned how to translate content statements into descriptions of student performances at a level of proficiency that would support the work of less experienced teachers attempting the same task. Throughout this first training session, lead teachers were mindful that they would become coaches in the planning process. When the principals and lead teachers completed their joint training, they were aware of the challenges that the SAPC would present to classroom teachers.

FIGURE 7.1

Agenda for Principal and Lead Teacher Training

Day 1

Morning
- Welcome by Dr. Castro, superintendent, followed by presentation of the district's policy for standards achievement and capacity-building efforts to support the role of administrators and educators
- Overview of the roles of principals and lead teachers in the district's curriculum reform efforts: advocacy, early support, and persistence

Afternoon
- *Principals:* Discussion of managing the allocation of time, print, and Internet resources to collaborative planning teams
- *Lead teachers:* Analysis of print and Internet resources as reference tools for standards planning

Day 2

Morning
- Presentation of the Standards Achievement Planning Cycle (SAPC), the central mechanism for standards achievement, and the conditions necessary for its success
- Introduction to standards-based planning: using standards planning tools to write instructional objectives

Afternoon
- Continuation of standards-based planning: using instructional objectives to evaluate student work samples through team collaboration

Day 3

Morning
- *Principals:* Review of advocacy guidelines to support the work of collaborating teams
- *Lead teachers:* Discussion of participation and advocacy within the SAPC: building trust and efficacy in planning groups

Afternoon
- Presentation of the SAPC rollout strategy, with guidance from curriculum leaders of the central office

---

Following leadership training, the lead teachers participated as team members in the professional development for classroom teachers, their second exposure to the SAPC. They helped the teachers acquire new skills during their training program, and they established themselves as facilitators and curriculum experts in the SAPC activities.

The professional development workshop helped school leaders plan the transition from teacher training to site-based implementation of the SAPC. Ongoing professional development and coordination of the leadership teams would be needed to monitor the success of SAPC implementation activities. Later in the year, school leaders received additional professional development in the use of the assessment system. As the first year of standards implementation came to a close, Mrs. Lewis attended a leadership institute to acquire the skills of the supervision process.

Initiating Professional Development for Teachers

The professional development program for teachers followed a full year of preparation by district and school leaders. All planning resources and enabling conditions described in Chapter 4 were put into place during this time. Principals and lead teachers received their training and shared their experiences with teachers along the way. The district's preparations for a standards-based curriculum were openly communicated with teachers and community members. Most important, the long-term plan and a time line for the complete rollout of the standards-based curriculum system was shared with the teachers and the community before the teachers received their professional development.

As the time for training approached, Mrs. Lewis told the teachers that they would attend four days of workshops. The agenda for teacher training is presented in Figure 7.2 on p. 142. The first two days of training would take place at the end of the school year, and the second two days would take place right before the start of the next school year. Through information sharing, the teachers knew a great deal about their responsibilities and the district's model for a standards-based curriculum prior to the first day of professional development in June. Anxiety about the program was substantially reduced because teachers were kept informed about the district's plans for a standards-based curriculum prior to the initial training.

Beginning the Training Program

At the start of teacher training, Mrs. Lewis and the lead teachers described the organization of the SAPC to their colleagues. Small

FIGURE 7.2

Agenda for Teacher Training

Day 1

Morning
- Welcome by Mrs. Lewis and the lead teachers at Mariposa Elementary School
- Presentation of the district's plan and time line for installing the new standards-based curriculum management system
- Overview of the new vision of teacher collaboration
- Description of new roles and responsibilities for administrators, lead teachers, and classroom teachers

Afternoon
- Presentation and modeling of the Standards Achievement Planning Cycle (SAPC) by Mrs. Lewis and lead teachers
- Discussion of each step of the SAPC and essential resources needed
- *Lead teachers:* Translation of selected content statements from the curriculum guide into performance descriptions
- *Grade-level teams:* Development of performance descriptions and comparison with sample standards-based lesson objectives prepared by lead teachers

Day 2

Morning
- Discussion of the implementation plan for the SAPC: how scheduling will be adjusted to accommodate more planning time and the rate and pace with which lessons will be planned collaboratively
- *Grade-level teams:* Review of new standards, frameworks, curriculum guide pacing information, and curriculum resources to be used in collaborative planning sessions
- Overview of the role and use of curriculum resources, including textbooks and activities, in standards-based planning

Afternoon
- Description of factors to consider in writing objectives for standards-based lessons
- *Grade-level teams:* Practice of the development of high-quality performance descriptions
- *Grade-level teams:* Completion of first draft of a standards-based lesson by the close of the afternoon
- Closing comments and distribution of evaluation forms for Days 1 and 2

Day 3

Morning
- Overview of the process and expectations for collaborative lesson planning, including discussion of logistics and schedules

FIGURE 7.2   (continued)

- *Grade-level teams:* Review of a high-quality standards-based lesson followed by review of draft lessons completed at the close of Day 2

Afternoon
- Overview of the process for team evaluation of student work samples
- Analysis of student work samples and lesson plans prepared and used by lead teachers in earlier leadership training
- *Grade-level teams:* Development of assessment activities for lesson objectives, and revision of lesson objectives to maximize their effectiveness as evaluative tools

Day 4

Morning
- *Grade-level teams:* Preparation of lesson plans for use in the evaluation of students' work; revision and improvement of student performance descriptions
- *Grade-level teams:* Planning for the first two weeks of collaboration, including the selection of standards to be addressed and resources to be used for developing learning activities

Afternoon
- Discussion of checklists and analytic rubrics for anticipated student reports and projects of the first unit to be taught through collaborative planning
- Presentation of the schedule for lesson production for the first two months of school
- Overview of upcoming continuing professional development in the use of the SAPC during the academic year
- Closing comments about support services that will be in place for each collaborative planning team

groups would work together throughout the academic year. At Mariposa, grade-level teams were organized for SAPC activities. Teachers were given the opportunity to ask questions about collaborative planning and their responsibility to the group process. They were encouraged to seek clarification, ask questions, and raise concerns about collaborative lesson planning and student work evaluation. These conversations included descriptions of the extensive preparations the district made to support collaboration.

The first day of the program featured a discussion of the long-term plan for implementing the curriculum management system. The time line included (1) the schedule for ongoing professional development during the academic year, (2) the introduction of the benchmark-testing program, and (3) the ultimate use of standards-based supervision methods following a long period of practice. The goal for the first morning of the program focused on full disclosure of the curriculum implementation plan, a presentation of the collaboration expectations for teachers, and a review of the responsibilities that administrators and lead teachers shared in the districtwide effort to improve student achievement. Mrs. Lewis and the lead teachers provided a thorough and patient presentation of the district's plans and expectations. This approach helped develop trust in the process and allowed the rest of the program to unfold in an environment of reduced anxiety.

The afternoon of the first day included a general overview of the SAPC as the central mechanism for standards achievement. Mrs. Lewis and her lead teachers described each step of the process, and working groups examined sample planning products that resulted from the stages of the SAPC. By the close of the first day, groups attempted their first exercise in identifying content statements from frameworks and translating one or two of these statements into performance descriptions. The groups then compared these descriptions with the objectives in model lessons appropriate to their teaching assignment.

During the second day of the program, teachers began an overview of the anticipated challenges that they would encounter in using the SAPC to plan lessons during the upcoming year. A large-group session at the start of the morning addressed important issues, including the rate at which standards-based lessons should be planned and taught during the year. Mrs. Lewis informed teachers that students would be released from school early on each Wednesday. Grade-level teams would meet to conduct the SAPC after students left the building. Mrs. Lewis told her teachers that the rate of lesson production would be slow at the outset. After two or three cycles of lesson planning and student work evaluation, teams would become efficient in the use of their time. The standards achievement pacing information and the new curriculum detailed the expected rate of lesson production.

Following the large-group discussion about lesson production expectations, the grade-level teams met in small groups with the assistance of Mrs. Hernandez and other lead teachers. During the meetings, the teachers reviewed their standards resource materials with their new knowledge of the SAPC. They discussed the strengths and limitations of the standards, frameworks, and adopted text materials as resources for standards-based lesson planning. Next, they reviewed the new curriculum guides prepared by curriculum leaders during the prior year. The guides described the scope and sequence of critical standards to be achieved in a given time.

The process of writing high-quality lesson objectives was the focus of the afternoon. The participants benefited from additional practice in writing performance descriptions from content statements. They focused on developing proficiency criteria that allow the lesson objectives to be used effectively in the evaluation of students' work. Mrs. Hernandez led this exercise, which culminated in groups reporting their progress and sharing examples of high-quality descriptions. Before the end of the day, each planning group completed a draft of its first standards-based lesson, which they would teach during the first week of school.

Mrs. Lewis closed the day's activities with a discussion of the important work to be done during the two training days before the start of the next school year. She told the teachers that standards-based lesson planning would get under way during the first week of school. Teachers would gain additional practice with SAPC activities in the upcoming training sessions, with an emphasis on using lesson objectives to evaluate students' work. Teachers filled out a professional development evaluation form at the end of the day to assess their sense of the efficacy of the lesson planning process. Concerns raised at the close of the second day were addressed at the start of the next professional development session.

Resuming the Training Program

The atmosphere of anticipation that typically envelops schools at the beginning of a new academic year was evident at Mariposa Elementary School as teachers started their second two-day professional development session. Interest in the SAPC as a new collaborative venture and the organization of teachers into learning communities made for a new beginning.

The first day of the final two days of training started with a review of the expectations and steps of the SAPC. Following small-group examination of model lessons with high-quality objectives, the teachers began refining the lesson plan that they developed in the previous two-day training session. Each group would teach this lesson in the first week of school.

The afternoon was dedicated to using lesson objectives for the evaluation of students' work. Mrs. Hernandez and the other lead teachers had planned and taught a standards-based lesson during the spring of the prior academic year in anticipation of this day in the professional development program. The lead teachers used the objectives of their lesson plan and three or four samples of resulting student work to demonstrate the evaluation process. During this session, the participants assessed each lesson objective as a tool for evaluating work samples, suggesting ways to better stimulate student achievement of the standard selected for the lesson. The activities closed with a workshop in which participants revised the proposed lesson objectives to make them more useful as evaluation tools.

During the last day of professional development before the start of the school year, collaborative groups were given substantial planning time to work on their first lesson, with an emphasis placed on using the lesson to evaluate students' work. They agreed that, on the first or second day of school, they would hold a collaborative planning session to evaluate student work samples that resulted from teaching their first standards-based lesson. Each team spent time looking at its lesson and unit plans from the past to form a collective strategy for teaching the critical standards that led up to the first benchmark assessment. Teams needed to feel confident that they had resources to apply the SAPC to each of the critical standards they were expected to achieve during the first several weeks of the academic year. In the afternoon, they discussed the process of writing analytic rubrics to evaluate instructional objectives for major projects that may be expected of students within the first 10 weeks of school.

As the final professional development day came to a close, Mrs. Lewis presented the schedule of grade-level meetings for the first two months of the school year. She told the teachers that they were not expected to demonstrate mastery of their new skills until they had conducted several cycles of the protocol. Additional professional development sessions would be held throughout the academic year focusing on the more challenging aspects of the SAPC, including (1) dealing with vague or broadly written standards, (2) writing performance descriptions that can easily discriminate between standards-meeting and substandard student work, (3) helping students who struggle with the new standards-based expectations, and (4) improving existing curriculum resources to elicit standards-meeting performances.

The teachers sensed that they were about to begin a group journey for the improvement of student achievement and that difficulties and challenges were to be expected along the way. They were comforted by Mrs. Lewis's description of technical assistance from the district and continuing support from lead teachers, as well as ongoing professional development sessions intended to address difficulties as they occurred.

Sustaining Momentum During the School Year

Soon after the school year started, Mrs. Lewis took the lead in sustaining the use of the SAPC. Mrs. Hernandez and the other lead teachers met regularly with Mrs. Lewis to monitor the early experiences of each planning team. The lead teachers checked with their colleagues to identify any problems that emerged. Mrs. Lewis stressed the importance of working collaboratively through informal conversations with individual teachers and in discussion with everyone during a faculty meeting at the end of the first month of school. Follow-up professional development sessions scheduled in the early autumn provided an opportunity for each planning team to see how others were coming along and to hear suggestions for overcoming commonly experienced challenges.

Looking Forward to the Second Year and Beyond

By the conclusion of the first semester, support services for collaborative planning groups became less essential and teachers grew more at ease with the new planning and evaluation activities. As comfort levels rose, the use of accountability tools entered the conversation.

Teachers learned that the benchmark-testing program would provide them with feedback regarding their collaborative evaluation of students' work. The tests were not intended to be a supervisory tool.

The supervision model was implemented in the second year of the program following extensive conversations with teachers about the SAPC. The building representative for the teachers' association was included in these discussions, and she informed teachers of the new observation procedures that had been negotiated with the district administration.

Lead teachers accepted the responsibility to provide new teaching staff with professional development in the SAPC. Through thoughtful interaction between Mrs. Lewis and her lead teachers, the SAPC eventually became routine practice, leading to academic excellence at Mariposa Elementary School.

Developing a Training Program for Your District

Dr. Castro and his colleagues invested a considerable amount of time in the planning of a professional development program for their district. The program included professional development experiences for everyone in the school district organization, including members of the board of education, central office leaders, school site leaders, and teachers. Principles of effective professional development were incorporated into the training experiences and the follow-up strategies that took place during the academic year. Figure 7.3 provides a checklist for school leaders who are responsible for creating a comprehensive professional development program in their districts.

FIGURE 7.3

Checklist for Professional Development Programs

The district's strategic plan for standards implementation includes professional development for all levels of the organization:

_____ school board members and district leaders

_____ principals, curriculum leaders, and lead teachers

_____ classroom teachers

FIGURE 7.3 (continued)

The districtwide professional development program includes school leaders and service providers:

_____ The district's strategic plan for standards implementation includes a time line for the professional development of principals, lead teachers, and classroom teachers.

_____ At all levels, professional development for standards implementation includes knowledge of the Standards Achievement Planning Cycle (SAPC), the district's plan for standards implementation, and collaborative work skills.

_____ Professional development for school board members and district leaders results in the adoption of district policies for standards implementation.

_____ Professional development for principals and school leaders is focused on their roles as support providers for teacher planning teams.

Essential resources for teacher professional development are procured and made available to planning groups prior to training:

_____ The district has identified the critical standards to be achieved at each grade level and for each core subject.

_____ Schedules have been adjusted to provide teachers with collaborative planning time during the course of the school day.

_____ Up-to-date state resources are available, including state standards, frameworks, and test blueprints.

_____ The district's curriculum guides have been updated to include standards pacing information.

_____ Up-to-date texts and other curriculum resources are aligned with district-selected critical standards.

_____ Professional development for teachers features the SAPC but also includes the use of instructional resources, group dynamics, and standards assessment tools.

_____ Initial professional development for teachers is followed by continuing support services from principals, curriculum leaders, and lead teachers.

_____ Principles of effective professional development are included in the training program for curriculum leaders and teachers, including coaching, guided practice, and feedback on implementation efforts.

_____ The professional development program provides teachers with time to develop standards achievement skills prior to the implementation of accountability measures.

Afterword

School districts from New Jersey to California have implemented many aspects of the SAPC as experienced by the fictional La Senda School District, but no one district has implemented them all. Nor should any district be expected to do so. Educators should adapt the ideas in this book to fit the specific policy and organizational environments where standards-based teaching and learning are needed. I offer the following messages to policymakers, school leaders, and teachers to aid them in a successful journey to standards achievement.

A Message to Policymakers

A comprehensive review of the professional literature concerning standards implementation preceded the description of standards-based teaching and learning in Chapter 2. The research was unequivocal regarding planning time for teachers: They simply must have more of it. Policymakers must take steps to communicate this requirement to school districts. No other resource will substitute for needed planning time.

Gradually, standards and frameworks must be revised to reflect the limited time available in the school year. States should not prescribe more standards than they can assess within a three-year rotating cycle of assessment. All required standards should be reasonably conveyed within an academic year, with sufficient time left over for local curriculum enhancement.

Standards, frameworks, and related state standards documents should be rewritten as resources for instructional planning. Content statements need to be accompanied by sample performance descriptions with qualifying language that characterizes a standards-meeting performance. Samples of exemplary student work with commentary should be made available on the Internet. Any teacher should be able to access a state-sponsored Web site that will provide the following resources for every standard that the state has mandated for achievement:

- background information that informs the teacher about the content and skills of the standard

- specific examples of student performances that will be expected on assessments of the standard

- released test items for each standard

- exercises and activities that will elicit performances that meet the standard

- clear descriptions of student performances that meet the standard

- specific explanations of which standards are tested, how frequently they are tested, the number of items used to assess the standard, and the relative weight of each standard for test-scoring purposes

The refusal of some state authorities to disclose this kind of information leaves teachers unsupported in their classrooms, and it is an invitation to failure.

Finally, state policymakers should revisit the idea of national standards for core content areas. Publishing companies could respond to national standards by providing many of the resources listed here. They cannot do this for separate sets of standards in each state.

A Message to School Leaders

Please be patient. It will take time for teachers to develop the trust and confidence to gain full value from the SAPC. Teachers will be able to address only a fraction of the standards in any one year. In two or three years, sufficient numbers of standards can be developed in each core curriculum area to lead to substantial growth in student achievement. Do not expect a world of change in student performance following one year. Please make every effort to identify with teachers as they take on the new roles of the SAPC. We are asking more of teachers these days than was ever asked of us when we started out in the profession.

A thorough standards-based lesson conveys knowledge in depth. Many standards will go untaught because there are too many standards to teach. Do not expect to see many standards-based lessons produced if only one extra hour of planning time is provided per week.

A Message to Teachers

The art of effective standards-based planning is one of envisioning student performances in detail, as if you were transported into the classroom during an anticipated lesson. Imagine that you can see every decision and action a student is making that demonstrates mastery of a standard. The next step is to describe those actions and their qualities as you make them the objectives of your lesson for all students to achieve. When you put faith in your ability to describe higher levels of student achievement suggested by the standards, you will lead your students to that destination.

Notes

Chapter 1

1. From California Department of Education (2003), p. 39. Copyright 2003 by California Department of Education, CDE Press, 1430 N Street, Suite 3207, Sacramento, CA 95814. Reprinted with permission.

2. From California Department of Education (2003), p. 44. Copyright 2003 by California Department of Education, CDE Press, 1430 N Street, Suite 3207, Sacramento, CA 95814. Reprinted with permission.

3. From California Department of Education (1999), p. 78. Copyright 1999 by California Department of Education, CDE Press, 1430 N Street, Suite 3207, Sacramento, CA 95814. Reprinted with permission.

Chapter 2

1. The identification of essential components of functional standards arose from the work of the New Standards Project, which has become New Standards under the direction of the National Center on Education and the Economy, 700 Eleventh Street NW, Suite 750, Washington, DC 20001.

2. Two informative resources concerning the new interest in evaluating students' work include the Looking at Student Work Web site at http://www.lasw .org and Allen and Blythe (2004).

3. From California Department of Education (2005), p. 54. Copyright 2005 by California Department of Education, CDE Press, 1430 N Street, Suite 3207, Sacramento, CA 95814. Reprinted with permission.

4. From California Department of Education (2005), p. 54. Copyright 2005 by California Department of Education, CDE Press, 1430 N Street, Suite 3207, Sacramento, CA 95814. Reprinted with permission.

Chapter 3

1. Copyright 2003 by California Department of Education, CDE Press, 1430 N Street, Suite 3207, Sacramento, CA 95814. Reprinted with permission.

2. Copyright 2003 by California Department of Education, CDE Press, 1430 N Street, Suite 3207, Sacramento, CA 95814. Reprinted with permission.

3. Copyright 1999 by California Department of Education, CDE Press, 1430 N Street, Suite 3207, Sacramento, CA 95814. Reprinted with permission.

4. Copyright 2003 by California Department of Education, CDE Press, 1430 N Street, Suite 3207, Sacramento, CA 95814. Reprinted with permission.

5. Other helpful resources include Mager (1984) and Gronlund (2003). Two Web sites that provide listings of action verbs sorted into the learning categories of Bloom's taxonomy are

- http://faculty.washington.edu/krumme/guides/bloom.html
- http://www.officeport.com/edu/blooms.htm

Chapter 4

1. The *California Standards for the Teaching Profession* were adopted by the California Department of Education and the California Commission on Teacher Credentialing in January 1997. A copy of the complete report describing each standard can be found at http://www.ctc.ca.gov/reports/CSTPreport.pdf.

2. The statement is found in the introduction to the standards available on the National Council for the Social Studies Web site at http://www.socialstudies .org/standards/strands/. Copyright 1994 by National Council for the Social Studies. Reprinted with permission.

3. Available from the New Jersey Department of Education at http://www .state.nj.us/njded/cccs/s6_ss.htm. Copyright 2004 by New Jersey Department of Education. Reprinted with permission.

4. The site index for the Web site of the Virginia Department of Education provides ease of access to all Commonwealth resources for standards-based planning, including standards, frameworks, blueprints, and test items: http://www.pen.k12.va.us/VDOE/siteindex/.

Chapter 6

1. Copyright 2005 by California Department of Education, CDE Press, 1430 N Street, Suite 3207, Sacramento, CA 95814. Reprinted with permission.

Chapter 7

1. A number of works on standards-based reform meet this description, including

- Anderson and Helms (2001): This study identifies a school's needs as it considers its future with standards. Standards implementation requires change in departments and schools, teacher collaboration in the work context, new student roles, and different kinds of student work. The authors conclude that research on interventions in conventional school practice is necessary, that attention needs to be given to teacher learning, and that the reform must be responsive to parental concerns.

• Bay (2000): In this study of standards implementation, the author identifies the challenges that can surface if all stakeholders are not brought into the planning and implementation process of standards reform. She also explores the conditions needed for an effective installation exercise.

• Black and William (1998): This article was one of the first analyses of the standards movement to focus on the need to describe the role of teachers and how they should proceed differently in a standards-based school.

• Corallo and McDonald (2001): The authors look at educational reform in relation to schools that have demonstrated dramatic improvement. They discuss the reform steps that are closely connected to improving schools and the role of standards in these schools.

• Guskey and Sparks (2002): Not all professional development reaches to the all-important level of meeting students' needs. This resource describes the characteristics of professional development that hold promise for helping teachers meet their students' needs more effectively.

• Lake, Hill, O'Toole, and Celio (1999): This resource describes how schools have organized to achieve educational reform goals and raise student achievement. The authors describe successful and unsuccessful efforts.

2. Readings on standards implementation, including the following, can help focus similar conversations on specific elements of proposed reforms:

• Lewis and Tsuchida (1998): Describing the process known as Japanese Lesson Study, the authors provide a thorough introduction to the possibility of improving instruction through collaborative lesson planning and instructional goal setting.

• Nave, Miech, and Mosteller (2000): This article identifies the need to include direct assistance to teachers for standards-based reforms. It sets the stage for the SAPC as a planning mechanism for the production of standards-based lessons and the evaluation of students' work.

• Ogawa, Sandholtz, Martinez-Flores, and Scribner (2003): This study makes clear that teachers need more than enabling resources and planning time to implement standards. The elements of an "instructional technology" are described, making way for the introduction of the SAPC.

• Resnick and Nolan (1995): In this policy study, the authors describe the important elements of instructional planning in an effective standards-based curriculum. Their explanation of the essential components of well-written, functional standards guided the development of the SAPC.

Bibliography

Allen, D., & Blythe, T. (2004). *The facilitator's book of questions: Tools for looking together at student and teacher work.* New York: Teachers College Press.

Anderson, R. D., & Helms, J. V. (2001). The ideal of standards and the reality of schools: Needed research. *Journal of Research in Science Teaching, 38*(1), 3–16.

Bay, J. M. (2000, April). *The dynamics of implementing and sustaining standards-based mathematics curricula in middle schools.* Paper presented at the annual meeting of the American Educational Research Association, New Orleans, LA.

Black, P., & William, D. (1998). Inside the black box: Raising standards through classroom assessment. *Phi Delta Kappan, 80*(2), 139–144, 146–148.

Bloom, B. S. (Ed.). (1956). *Taxonomy of educational objectives: The classification of educational goals. Handbook 1. Cognitive domain.* New York: Longmans, Green.

California Department of Education. (1999). *Reading/language arts framework for California public schools.* Sacramento: Author.

California Department of Education. (2003). *Science framework for California public schools.* Sacramento: Author.

California Department of Education. (2005). *History–social science framework for California public schools.* Sacramento: Author.

Carle, E. (2001). *The very hungry caterpillar.* New York: Penguin Putnam.

Commonwealth of Virginia Department of Education. (2002). *Mathematics standards of learning: Sample scope and sequence algebra I.* Richmond: Author.

Commonwealth of Virginia Department of Education. (2003). *Blueprint, grade 5, mathematics test.* Richmond: Author.

Commonwealth of Virginia Department of Education. (2004). *Virginia department of education web site index.* Retrieved December 1, 2004, from http://www.pen.k12.va.us/VDOE/siteindex/

Corallo, C., & McDonald, D. (2001). *What works with low-performing schools: A review of research literature on low-performing schools.* Washington, DC: Office of Educational Research and Improvement.

Falk, B. (2000). *The heart of the matter: Using standards and assessment to learn.* New York: Heinemann.

Gibbons, S., Kimmel, H., & O'Shea, M. (1997). Changing teacher behavior through staff development: Implementing the teaching and content standards in science. *School Science and Mathematics, 97*(6), 302–309.

Gronlund, N. E. (2003). *Writing instructional objectives for teaching and assessment* (7th ed.). Upper Saddle River, NJ: Prentice Hall.

Guskey, T. R. (1986). Staff development and the process of teacher change. *Educational Researcher, 15,* 5–12.

Guskey, T. R. (2003). What makes professional development effective? *Phi Delta Kappan, 84*(10), 748–750.

Guskey, T. R., & Sparks, D. (2002, April). *Linking professional development to improvements in student learning.* Paper presented at the annual meeting of the American Educational Research Association, New Orleans, LA.

Harris, D. E., & Carr, J. F. (1996). *How to use standards in the classroom.* Alexandria, VA: Association for Supervision and Curriculum Development.

Haycock, K. (1998). Good teaching matters . . . a lot. *Thinking K–16, 3*(2), 3–14.

Lake, R. J., Hill, P. T., O'Toole, L., & Celio, M. B. (1999). *Making standards work: Active voices, focused learning.* Seattle: Center on Reinventing Public Education, University of Washington.

Lewis, C., & Tsuchida, I. (1998, Winter). A lesson is like a swiftly flowing river: How research lessons improve Japanese education. *American Educator, 22*(4), 12–17, 50–52.

Mager, R. F. (1984). *Preparing instructional objectives* (Rev. 2nd ed.). Belmont, CA: Pitman Management and Training.

Marzano, R. (1998). *Implementing standards-based education.* Washington, DC: National Education Association.

Marzano, R., & Kendall, J. (1996). *A comprehensive guide to designing standards-based districts, schools, and classrooms.* Alexandria, VA: Association for Supervision and Curriculum Development.

National Commission on Mathematics and Science Teaching for the 21st Century. (2000). *Before it's too late.* Jessup, MD: U.S. Department of Education.

National Council for the Social Studies. (1994). *Expectations of excellence: Curriculum standards for social studies.* Silver Spring, MD: Author.

National Research Council. (1995). *National science education standards.* Washington, DC: National Academy Press.

Nave, M., Miech, E., & Mosteller, F. (2000). A lapse in standards: Linking standards-based reform with student achievement. *Phi Delta Kappan, 82*(2), 128–132.

New Jersey Department of Education. (2004). *Core curriculum content standards for social studies.* Trenton: Author.

Ogawa, R., Sandholtz, J. H., Martinez-Flores, M., & Scribner, S. P. (2003). The substantive and symbolic consequences of a district's standards-based curriculum. *American Educational Research Journal, 40*(1), 147–176.

O'Shea, M. (2002). Teaching to standards. *Thrust for Leadership, 31*(3), 22–37.

O'Shea, M., & Kimmel, H. (2003, January). *Preparing teachers for content standards: A field study of implementation problems.* Paper presented at the annual meeting of the American Association for Colleges of Teacher Education, New Orleans, LA.

Reeves, D. (1998). *Making standards work: How to implement standards-based assessments in the classroom, school, and district.* Denver, CO: Center for Performance Assessment.

Resnick, L. B., & Nolan, K. L. (1995). Standards for education. In D. Ravitch (Ed.), *Debating the future of American education: Do we need national standards and assessments?* (pp. 94–119). Washington, DC: Brookings Institution.

Scherer, M. (2001, September). How and why standards can improve student achievement: A conversation with Robert J. Marzano. *Educational Leadership, 59*(1), 14–18.

Skinner, R. A., & Staresina, L. N. (2004, January 8). State of the states. *Education Week, 17*(23), 97–153.

Tell, C., Bodone, F., & Addie, K. (2000, April). *A framework of teacher knowledge and skills necessary in a standards-based system: Lessons from high school and university faculty.* Paper presented at the annual meeting of the American Educational Research Association, New Orleans, LA.

Wiggins, G., & McTighe, J. (1998). *Understanding by design.* Alexandria, VA: Association for Supervision and Curriculum Development.

Willis, S. (2002, March). Creating a knowledge base for teaching: A conversation with James Stigler. *Educational Leadership, 59*(6), 6–11.

Zmuda, A., & Tomaino, M. (2001). *The competent classroom: Aligning high school curriculum, standards, and assessment—A creative teaching guide.* Washington, DC: National Education Association; and New York: Teachers College Press.

Index

In this index, page locators followed by *f* indicate information found in figures or sidebars.

assessment. *See also* instructional supervision
  criterion-referenced standards-based tests, 64
  norm-referenced vs. criterion-referenced tests, 126–127
  for standards achievement, 106–116, 122–129, 128–129*f*
  standards-based vs. standardized tests, 41*f*
  state standards tests, 40–41, 51*f*, 124–127
assessment, classroom-based. *See also* benchmark testing; instructional supervision
  checklists for, 113–114, 114*f*
  direct engagement with standards, 112
  incorporating into lesson planning, 6–8, 107–110, 114*f*
  performance descriptions in, 109–111
  rubrics for, 114–115
  of student performance or products, 35, 57–59, 110–111
  tools for, alternative and metacognitive, 111–113

benchmark testing, 12–13, 38–40, 115–124, 118–121*f*. *See also* assessment; standards achievement
black box model, 19, 21–23, 21*f*

Bloom's taxonomy with behavioral verbs, 53*f*
Bush, George H. W., 1

classroom, example of standards-based, 2–14
community involvement, 39, 66, 95–96
content statements, 51*f*
curriculum guides, 37, 76–82, 80*f*, 83*f*, 116
curriculum management. *See also* lesson plans
  district strategies in, 15–19
  evaluating, 123–127
  example of Mariposa Elementary, 1–14
  materials selection in, 17–18, 37–38, 38*f*, 82–87
  SAPC emergence in, 25–27
  standards implementation strategies, 19–23, 20*f*, 21*f*
  standards-meeting protocols, 23–25

district assessment coordinators, 40–41
district role in standards implementation. *See also* professional development
  assessment checklist, 128–129*f*
  benchmark testing, 12–13, 115–124, 118–121*f*
  communications plan, 39, 62–68

district role in standards implementation (*continued*)
   curriculum policy, 15–19, 37, 76–82, 80*f*, 83*f*, 116
   implementation checklist, 87–88*f*
   leadership, 39, 131–135, 150–152
   materials selection, 17–18, 37–38, 38*f*, 82–87
   reform agenda development, 67–68, 68*f*
   research documentation, 65–66
   standards selection process, 70–76, 71*f*
   support functions, 23, 38, 42, 68–70

Elementary and Secondary Education Act, 1
evaluation of standards achievement. *See under* assessment

instructional planning. *See* curriculum management; lesson plans
instructional supervision. *See also* assessment; teachers in standards-based schools
   cycle of, 96
   lesson observation and assessment, 10–11, 99–101, 100*f*
   postobservation assessment, 101–104
   postobservation conferences, 11, 102–103
   postobservation expectations, 101–102
   preobservation assessment, 97–99, 98*f*
   preobservation expectations, 97–99, 98*f*

Japanese Lesson Study, 24–25

leadership. *See* lead teachers; principals in standards-based schools; *under* district role in standards implementation
lead teachers, 91–92, 136–141, 140*f*
learning activities
   preobservation evaluation of, 97
   selection and sequencing, 34–35, 55–57, 57*f*
lesson objectives, 2–7, 3–4*f*, 97
lesson plans. *See also* curriculum management
   activities and objectives development, 34–35, 51–57, 57*f*

lesson plans (*continued*)
   assessment, incorporating into, 8, 107–110, 114*f*
   assessment criteria, 100*f*
   collaborative development of, 8–9, 38, 68–70, 90, 93
   conventional vs. standards-based, 27–32
   examples, 2–6, 3–4*f*, 27*f*, 29–31*f*, 57*f*
   importance in SAPC, 25–26
   Japanese Lesson Study model, 24–25
   preobservation assessment, 97–99, 98*f*
   resource planning, 56
   time requirements, 38, 59–60, 68–70, 90, 93
Looking at Student Work, 25

No Child Left Behind, 1

performance descriptions, 109–111
planning cycle. *See* Standards Achievement Planning Cycle (SAPC)
principals in standards-based schools
   as advocates, 39
   as advocates for reform, 137–138
   as change agents, 89–92
   checklist of practices, 14*f*
   community involvement by, 95–96
   example of Mariposa Elementary, 9–11
   as leaders, 94–95, 104–105*f*
   superintendent interactions, 93–94
   as support system for
      curriculum management, 91–92, 138
      installation success, 92–96
      planning process, 90, 93, 96–104, 138–141
   union negotiations by, 96–97, 99
professional development. *See also* district role in standards implementation
   adult learning principles in, 132
   creating effective, 135–136
   for district leaders, 131–135
   example of Mariposa Elementary, 9–11
   importance of, 18–19
   for lead teachers, 136–141, 140*f*
   planning for, 90, 92, 130–131
   for principals, 136–141, 140*f*
   program checklist, 148–149*f*

professional development (*continued*)
  sustaining momentum, 147
  for teachers, 141–148, 142–143*f*

schools, standards-based
  checklist of practices, 13–14*f*
  developing, 9–13
  Mariposa Elementary example, 2–9
schools, underperforming, 22
standards
  analysis of, 33, 49–51
  enduring, 72–74
  identification of, 32–33, 46–49
  process vs. content, 47, 51*f*
  state-level, benefits of, 63–64
  tested, 74–76
standards achievement. *See also*
  benchmark testing; state standards
  tests
  black box model, 19, 21–23, 21*f*
  common strategies for, 15–19, 20*f*
  evaluating, 42–43, 43–44*f*, 106–116,
    122–129, 128–129*f*
  Japanese Lesson Study model,
    24–25
  Looking at Student Work process,
    25
  planning protocols for, 22–25
  professional development for,
    18–19
  textbooks and, 17–19, 37, 38*f*, 64
Standards Achievement Planning
  Cycle (SAPC)
  components of, 26–27
  enabling conditions, 35–39, 36*f*,
    150–152
  premises essential to, 25–26
  school readiness checklist, 60–61*f*
  sustaining conditions, 39–42,
    96–104, 147, 151
Standards Achievement Planning
  Cycle (SAPC) steps
  1. identify standards to be
    addressed, 32–33, 46–49
  2. analyze selected standards and
    frameworks, 33, 49–51
  3. describe student performances
    or products, 33–34, 51–55, 53f

Standards Achievement Planning
  Cycle (SAPC) steps (*continued*)
  4. select and sequence learning
    activities, 34–35, 55–57, 57*f*
  5. evaluate student performances
    or products, 35, 43*f*, 57–59
standards implementation
  common strategies, 19–23, 20*f*, 21*f*
  enabling conditions, 35–39, 36*f*,
    150–152
  evaluating, 13–14*f*, 43–44*f*
  sustaining conditions, 39–42
standards selection, essential vs.
  excessive, 70–76, 71*f*
state-level standards, benefits of,
  63–64
state standards tests, 40–41, 51*f*,
  124–127. *See also* standards
  achievement
student performance or products,
  33–35, 51–59, 53*f*, 109–111

teacher observation. *See* instructional
  supervision
teachers in standards-based schools.
  See also instructional supervision
  checklist of practices, 13–14*f*
  collaborative planning by, 38,
    59–60, 68–70, 90, 93
  developing, 9–11
  implementation advice to, 152
  lead teachers, 91–92, 136–141, 140*f*
  resources essential to, 22–23,
    36–37
  setting learning expectations, 26
teaching to the test, 26
test blueprints, 75. *See also* assessment
testing. *See* assessment
textbooks, standards-aligned, 17–19,
  37, 38*f*, 64
theory of action, 22
time requirements for collaborative
  planning, 38, 59–60, 68–70, 90, 93

Understanding by Design (Wiggins &
  McTighe), 72–73
union negotiations in protocol development, 96–97, 99

About the Author

Photo by Wayne Capili

Mark R. O'Shea is a professor of education at California State University–Monterey Bay. He is the founder and executive director of the Institute for the Achievement of Academic Standards. O'Shea received a bachelor's degree from the University of Virginia, an MAT degree from the University of Chicago, and an EdD from Teachers College, Columbia University. He has taught science in public high schools of Pennsylvania, New York, and New Jersey and has served as a school supervisor and board of education trustee. For the last 20 years, he has been an administrator and faculty member in colleges and universities in Virginia, Colorado, New Jersey, and California.

Since 1996, O'Shea has been studying the standards movement from the perspective of the classroom teacher. He has conducted extensive clinical research in standards-based teaching in association with Howard Kimmel of the New Jersey Institute of Technology. O'Shea has written articles on standards-based teaching, has presented at numerous professional conferences, and has consulted with school districts and state departments of education. He may be reached at mark_oshea@csumb.edu or at California State University–Monterey Bay, 100 Campus Center, Bldg. 84E, Seaside, CA 93955. Additional resources for implementing the standards achievement strategies in this book can be found at http://www.academicstandards.org.

Related ASCD Resources: Standards

At the time of publication, the following ASCD resources were available; for the most up-to-date information about ASCD resources, go to www.ascd.org. ASCD stock numbers are noted in parentheses.

Audio

Making Standards Manageable by Elliott Asp (2 Audiotapes #202105)

Strategic Planning for Standards-Based Systems by Charles Schwahn (2 Audiotapes #202093)

Supervision in a Standards-Based World by Judy Carr (Audiotape #204166; CD #504300)

Unpacking Standards: Taking the High Road by Lynn Erickson (Audiotape #202100)

Mixed Media

Implementing Standards-Based Education: Professional Inquiry Kit by Jane Ellison and Carolee Hayes (#999222)

Networks

Visit the ASCD Web site (www.ascd.org) and click on About ASCD. Go to the section on Networks for information about professional educators who have formed groups around topics such as "Learning and Assessment" and "Restructuring Schools." Look in the Network Directory for current facilitators' addresses and phone numbers.

Online Courses

Visit the ASCD Web site (www.ascd.org) for the following professional development opportunities:

Crafting Curriculum by Kathy Checkley (#PD03OC26)

Creating Standards-Based Curricula by Angelika Machi (#PD03OC34)

Print Products

A Comprehensive Guide to Designing Standards-Based Districts, Schools, and Classrooms by Robert J. Marzano and John S. Kendall (#196215)

Educational Leadership, September 2001: Making Standards Work (Entire Issue #101271)

Meeting Standards Through Integrated Curriculum by Susan M. Drake and Rebecca C. Burns (#103011)

Standards Topic Pack (#104468; also available in electronic format #104468E)

Succeeding with Standards: Linking Curriculum, Assessment, and Action Planning by Judy F. Carr and Douglas E. Harris (#101005)

Teaching What Matters Most: Standards and Strategies for Raising Student Achievement by Richard W. Strong, Harvey F. Silver, and Matthew J. Perini (#100057)

Video

Examining Student Work Series Tapes 1–4: *Improving Student Learning, The Tuning Protocol, Standards in Practice™ (SIP), Collaborative Analysis of Student Learning* (4 Videotapes and Facilitator's Guide #401283)

Using Standards to Improve Teaching and Learning Series Tapes 1–3: *Improving Roles and School Structure, Improving Curriculum and Assessment, Improving Classroom Instruction* (3 Videotapes and Facilitator's Guide #400262)

For more information, visit us on the World Wide Web (www.ascd.org), send an e-mail message to member@ascd.org, call the ASCD Service Center (1-800-933-ASCD or 703-578-9600, then press 2), send a fax to 703-575-5400, or write to Information Services, ASCD, 1703 N. Beauregard St., Alexandria, VA 22311-1714 USA.